Rediscovering the Spirit

Rediscovering the Spirit

From Political Brokenness to Spiritual Wholeness

Lowell Greathouse

WIPF & STOCK · Eugene, Oregon

REDISCOVERING THE SPIRIT
From Political Brokenness to Spiritual Wholeness

Wipf & Stock
An Imprint of Wipf and Stock Publishers
199 W. 8th Ave., Suite 3
Eugene, OR 97401

www.wipfandstock.com

PAPERBACK ISBN: 978-1-7252-8520-0
HARDCOVER ISBN: 978-1-7252-8521-7
EBOOK ISBN: 978-1-7252-8522-4

Manufactured in the U.S.A.   10/13/20

To Susan, my life companion, and to all those who have brought joy, challenge, and insight to enrich the journey.

Contents

Acknowledgements | ix

Introduction: From Political Brokenness to Spiritual Wholeness | xiii

Part I: The Journey Begins Within | 1

1. Measuring What We Are Really Worth:
   Spiritual Principles and Moral Markers | 7

2. An Inward-Out Movement | 14

Part II: Four Qualities of Spiritual Wholeness | 19

3. Centering: Grounding and Seeing Reality with Clarity | 22

4. Framing: Making Sense of the World | 35

5. Practicing: Turning Spiritual Principles into Personal Habits | 47

6. Living with Others: Engaging Life with Wholeness | 65

Part III: Navigating Times of Political Turmoil | 87

7. Barriers to Making Progress in Our Spiritual Journey | 89

8. Recovering the Spirit in Times of Political Peril:
   Addressing Exceptionalism, Originalism, Marketplace Culture,
   and Trumpism | 108

9. Dealing with Conflict: Coming Together When
   Things Are Falling Apart | 124

10. Vocation: Discovering Life's Calling | 128

Epilogue | 133

Bibliography | 143

Contents

Acknowledgements

REDISCOVERING THE SPIRIT IS the result of much more than just putting words in a book. It is the culmination of countless hours of conversation, significant life experiences shared with others, and a number of epiphanies and serendipities that have taken place along the way. Because of this, there are a number of people who simply must be acknowledged and thanked for their part in bringing *Rediscovering the Spirit* to fruition.

First and foremost, I owe special thanks to my wife and life partner, Susan. We have shared life together for nearly forty years, beginning with our trip to the Honduran border with El Salvador and Guatemala as an international delegation to the refugee camps located there in 1982. Thanks to her insights, willingness to be a sounding board for my ideas, and her ongoing spirit of adventure, I have grown as a person and as a writer over the years, even as we have grown together as a couple. Raising a family and having two thoughtful, caring daughters in Lindsey and Kelly, represent the deep joy of our journey.

I am also grateful for having had two amazing parents who helped me think about life more deeply, as well as be socially aware, from the very beginning. Many of the things I have focused attention on in this book are the result of watching and learning from them years ago. Part of this work is also the result of many hours of conversation with my two brothers, Mark and Gordon, who share many of the same concerns that I discuss in *Rediscovering the Spirit*. In these ways, this book is a kind of family album.

I have been blessed by having a number of remarkable work settings in which I was able to live out my deepest values. I also had many teachers along the way, who inspired me and guided my thought development and spiritual growth throughout life. These teachers and mentors include John Whiteneck, Doug Nelson, Jim Barlow, John Roth, John Snortum, Alpheus Mason, Mary Harris, Marvin Chandler, Richard Foster, Rene Pino, among many others. It is a gift, beyond words, to have mentors and guides who are willing to share their experiences and perspectives.

My research and study for this book has also been deeply influenced by important historical figures who have helped shape my understanding of life, including Abraham Lincoln, Mohandas Gandhi, Jesus, Harriet Tubman, Albert Schweitzer, Howard Thurman, Oscar Romero, John Howard Griffin, Martin Luther King Jr., Robert Kennedy, Sergio Mendez Arceo, Nelson Mandela, John Wesley, Henri Nouwen, Paulo Freire, and others. Their life journeys have helped me shape my own understanding of the world in ways that have influenced how I approach spiritual and political matters.

Studying theology, civil society, human psychology, and spiritual dynamics first at Claremont McKenna College as an undergraduate and then at San Francisco Theological Seminary and Azusa Pacific University provided me with important settings, colleagues, and teachers to test my ideas and learn from others about spirituality and the interplay between personal and social settings. I am also grateful for having attended the Parliament of the World's Religions on two occasions, in Melbourne, Australia in 2009 and in Toronto, Canada in 2018, so that I could learn from some of the best minds throughout the world, who represent so many different religious and cultural traditions. These experiences were true learning laboratories for developing the kind of spiritual life I discuss throughout this book.

Over the years, I have been blessed to be a part of many cross-cultural experiences. These experiences have not only shaped my understanding of life in profound ways, but have challenged my assumptions while deepening my spirit. This book would not be the same had I not had so many rich and varied opportunities outside my own cultural background. I have been blessed to learn about cultural differences at an early age and be part of a cross-cultural family, but was also fortunate to work with children from various cultural backgrounds in New York many years ago. Having the chance to live and work in Cuernavaca, Mexico, while in seminary and be with so many colleagues from various cultures over the years has deeply influenced how I see politics and spirituality. I have had many insightful teachers and friends who opened my eyes throughout my journey.

Because *Rediscovering the Spirit* is fundamentally about how one approaches life, I would be remiss if I didn't mention the names of those who have been a part of important conversations over the years. They include Devon Hartman, Mary Beierle, Mike Smith, Sharon Powers, Kenny Wood, colleagues from my work at Oregon Fair Share, Catholic Charities of San Francisco, Community Action in Washington County, and United Way of the Columbia-Willamette, as well as so many friends and parishioners from the United Methodist Church in Filer, Idaho, and in Lake Oswego, Beaverton, Portland First in Oregon, as well as colleagues from the Greater Northwest Area Cabinet of the UMC. Each of these settings informed what I learned about centering, framing, practicing, and living with others as a part of my own faith journey. My friends and colleagues have always been patient with my limitations and generous with their insights.

I have gained a great deal from being a part of the Writers in the Grove group in Forest Grove, Oregon. This talented, supportive community of writers has helped me grow as both a writer and a person. Mary Jane Nordgren's guidance of this weekly gathering of writers has created a setting that inspires good writing and establish an environment of thoughtful critique among us.

I am grateful to the Wipf and Stock publishing team for their support and work with me as a first-time author. Their experience, encouragement, and skill have been instrumental to bringing this effort to fruition.

Finally, I'm thankful for those who read and provided helpful feedback to the earlier versions of my manuscript, including Frank Rogers, Dave Richardson, Julia Nielsen, Ann Farley, Mike Smith, Gordon Greathouse, and my wife, Susan.

It is clear to me that a book such as this does not happen in a vacuum. It is the culmination of many people's insights and experiences. I deeply value being a part of such an amazing community of friends, colleagues, and family.

Introduction

From Political Brokenness to Spiritual Wholeness

IMAGINE FOR A MOMENT what it would be like to stand at an intersection and observe the aftermath of a tragic accident. There is a lot of damage to take in. There are people calling out for help. Some are running to assist, while others are running away. There is a lot to see. At moments like this, we discover what we are truly made of.

Today we stand at a critical crossroads as witnesses to an awful set of circumstances that have created widespread frustration and social dysfunction. In all the confusion, we have lost track of many of the spiritual essentials that give life meaning and connect us with each other. It is time to intervene, change our ways, and do something different, significant, and bold.

Something important has happened, and we can no longer ignore the ramifications that have been exposed. We see the evidence in our politics and economics, but the most lasting impact has taken place within us—spiritually—as we try to make sense of our world and live our lives. This situation has evolved in recent years, as we continue to neglect the fundamentals of spirituality and underestimate their importance to our future. We do so at our collective peril.

If this wasn't clear before, in the spring of 2020 the realities involved at this critical crossroads were exposed in powerful ways as longstanding racism and institutional injustice were revealed through the murder of George Floyd by Minneapolis police officers, as a major pandemic swept across the globe, as unemployment reached levels not seen since the Great Depression, and as governmental and religious leadership failed in many ways to be a positive agent of change, reconciliation, and social advancement. Yes, we are at a critical crossroads where a tragic accident has taken place, and it is not just political in nature. It is deeply spiritual, as well. What happens next depends on all of us.

It is time to name and address these matters head on, step back to reflect on what has happened, and then proceed to find a new way forward that honors spiritual realities and longstanding wisdom teachings. *Rediscovering the Spirit* is an attempt to do this by reframing our current national crisis and division along spiritual, rather than political, fault lines. Even if the political warfare in the United States were to cease immediately, we would not be out of our current turmoil. If we do not reorient our spiritual lives in healthier ways, we simply will not heal our individual and collective souls, nor make progress as a nation.

Fortunately, what many refer to as "spirit" continues to be very much alive and present in the world, even if we are not accessing its value fully. We depend upon spiritual understandings to give meaning to our days, provide a framework for our view of the world, and sustain us in difficult, turbulent times. At the crossroads where we currently find ourselves, we need to make a crucial turn and venture forth in a new direction.

For years, I've had the words "only those who can see the invisible can accomplish the impossible"[1] displayed in my office. These words remind me about the importance of paying attention to those things that, while at first are invisible to the naked eye, describe the essentials we need in order to navigate our material world in meaningful ways.

Spirituality is at the heart of what it means to be a human being who is fully alive. Countless religions and faith traditions demonstrate this essential truth. Our time on earth is about both the ticking of the clock and the beating of the heart, about physical reality and spiritual presence. As human beings, we have a deep desire for life to have meaning and substance. To be alive is to experience the world through the senses and be aware of how our heart and mind process these experiences, attaching value and purpose to them. These are the "invisible" components of living. Spirit is the mortar that ultimately holds things together and gives them shape and value.

Our world is made up of material things, and we need to pay attention to them in order to function on a daily basis. But all too often, we get caught up in the material world and in the politics that define us in a given time and place. If we aren't aware of the importance and presence of the spiritual realm that infuses all of life with meaning, we will neither understand nor

---

1. Author unknown. This quote has been attributed to a variety of different sources from Jeffrey Fry to Frank Gaines. Its origin is difficult to determine.

appreciate the totality of our existence. Failing to attend to the invisible dynamics in creation makes it nearly impossible to discover wholeness and integrity as individuals or as a society.

In the fall of 2019, my wife, Susan, and I made a seven-week 9,500-mile journey, driving across the United States and visiting some twenty-five states. During our travels, we saw a number of remarkable, inspiring sites that depict our nation's story and reflect its natural beauty. We were often surprised by the spiritual dynamics that were a part of many of these experiences.

In Memphis, Tennessee, we visited the Lorraine Motel and the National Civil Rights Museum located there. Much could be written about the power of this museum and the story it tells about the history of the African-American experience in our nation. The site is filled with pictures, displays, and stories that depict the long, harrowing journey of this community through American history. It moves from the hardships and suffering of slavery through the inspiration and accomplishment of the Civil Rights Movement. It is a place immersed in the physical realities and the political turmoil that was a part of this long history.

When we came to the end of the exhibit, we found ourselves standing at the actual room (Room 306), where Dr. Martin Luther King Jr. spent his last hours. It was a very ordinary physical space with two beds, a nightstand, and dresser. There we found ourselves standing just a few feet from the place where he was shot and killed. It was here where I experienced something much more powerful than simply a personal reaction to what was in front of me physically. Suddenly, I moved to a spiritual, transcendent place where I reflected on Dr. King's life and witness.

It was as if I could hear the words he'd spoken the night before at the Bishop Charles Mason Temple Church of God:

> I don't know what will happen now. We've got some difficult days
> ahead. But it really doesn't matter with me now. Because I've been
> to the mountaintop. And I don't mind. Like anybody, I would like
> to live a long life. Longevity has its place. But I'm not concerned
> about that now. I just want to do God's will.[2]

Then a series of questions flooded in: What took place within Dr. King's life to lead him from the comforts of seminary in Boston to the segregated South in the first place? How was he able to speak out against social

---

2. Ellis and Smith, *Say It Plain*, 86.

injustice and racial oppression against such great odds? Where did he find the inner resources he needed to risk his life on behalf of others for so many years? How did he find the courage to make his way to Memphis, Tennessee, and the Lorraine Motel in the spring of 1968?

Dr. King must have known that he could die at any time because of his convictions and willingness to stand up for freedom, justice, and human rights. As we stood there, these were the questions that this place of holy ground invited me to grapple with. It is why spirituality, which is inner work, always proceeds the actions and physical activities that are a part of our lives.

As we left the Lorraine Motel, there was still more to our experience at the National Civil Rights Museum. After standing at Room 306, we walked across the street, where the museum continued in a small building located there. It was the boarding house where James Earl Ray rented a room in April 1968 and at 6 pm on April 4th raised his Remington rifle and assassinated Dr. Martin Luther King Jr.

I had an eerie feeling in this place. Here I was looking out a boarding house window onto the balcony in front of Room 306 across the street. That was the spot where Dr. King stood in 1968 when he was assassinated. It was through this window that Ray positioned King in the scope of his rifle and pulled the trigger. Standing there, I felt death lingering in the air all these years later.

The whole experience reminded me of something I heard Daniel Berrigan say in a seminary class I attended: "Who dies first, the killer or the victim?" It is a rather strange question on one level, but when you reflect on it, you realize that this powerful question is about one's inner spirit.

What happened moments earlier at the Lorraine Motel where Dr. King died, happened again at the boarding house window. Now I was pondering these questions: Who was James Earl Ray at this point in his life? What had happened to his spirit prior to April 4th that led him to take the life of a man standing across the street? How did his inner darkness lead him to raise the barrel of a gun that evening and change the course of human history?

Spirituality is about these kinds of deep questions. They are questions related to the good and evil that dwells within us. Our responses to these inner questions determine who we become and how we spend our lives in the material, political world.

It is in the spiritual realm where we grapple with the critical existential questions of life:

- Who am I? And who are we?
- Why am I here? And what are we called to be collectively?
- How shall I live? And how shall we live together as neighbors?

These are the issues that take us on a journey in which we explore the spiritual life and determine why our time on earth matters.

When I look at my own life, the spirit reflects those hidden life forces that impel, compel, inspire, and draw me toward certain people, events, and physical realities. I can't explain these things through simple logic, material well-being, or return on investment. They simply matter inside—at the heart of who I am. They are the essentials that bring harmony or dissonance to my very being. They affirm life, connect me to others, and produce joy and meaning in my life.

Why reach out to a stranger in need or become interested in someone who is different from me? Why give time, energy, and money to causes I'll get no material return from, or stand in nature's beauty and have nothing better to say than "Thank you," instead of "I wish I owned this"? Why shed tears when inspired by someone's kindness or be moved to risk one's life for a seemingly impossible cause?

This is the stuff of spirituality. Spirit is about remembering people and stories years later because they inspire or touch with special meaning. Why remember some people who are a part of those stories rather than others?

Spirit is the common thread that holds life events and experiences together in a special way and defines those things that matter most in life and make it worth living. It is about what I'm willing to invest in and give my life for. These are the stories we pass on to our children and our children's children. It is what we hold most dear.

The nature of one's spirit determines whether you discover your better angels and come to Memphis in April 1968 to speak out against injustice and oppression or whether you lose your way, diminish your spirit, and go to Memphis to take someone else's life. It is a movement that travels inside out, from spirit to the social, political world.

Spirit is about such things. It doesn't fit neatly on a balance sheet. It can't be put in a box, explained in a tweet, or be captured in a simple definition. This is why matters of the heart are so difficult to put into words. Spirit is what brings tears to our eyes and invites us to say "I love you" to someone else. Not everyone calls these things by spiritual-sounding names, but in the end, we are pointing to the same things, which we cherish and give special value to in our lives.

Spirit is often communicated better through poetry and song rather than through facts and figures or prose.

Spirit Alive

How can there be what we cannot see?
Is it because spirit comes with the first breath of life,
then vanishes into thin air,
taking flight until the very last moment we share?

Is spirit the light that shines beyond words?
The transcendence that takes us beyond here?
There are times when spirit appears on a cheek,
as a tear shedding sorrow, joy, wonder.

Is spirit what comes through our love for each other,
as communion, connection, and union run free?
Is spirit as ancient as the Greek's *pneuma* or the Hebrew's *ruach*?
Perhaps it arrived before they were here.

Maybe spirit's been present, alive all along.
It's just we've not noticed; it's so hard to see.

How can spirit be essence and memory,
traveling through time and class so effortlessly?
It is spirit that's shared one to another,
passed down, word of mouth, through the ages.
It's the nudge that pushes us one toward another,
becoming friends bound together through time.

Spirit is the story of life's deepest yearnings,
giving shape to the things we hold dear.
Perhaps spirit is the breath we were given at birth,
then it dwells in the place where we learn how to live.

The truth is we have two fundamental hungers as human beings. The first is for the food we need to sustain our bodies. The second is the hunger to experience life fully so there is meaning to our time on earth. These human instincts both need to be nourished. If one or the other is ignored, we get indigestion within or worse. What we see physically matters, but what we experience spiritually is critical as well. When we neglect our spiritual lives, we become out of sorts and imbalanced. This is reflected in both personal and social ways.

The situation regarding the recent novel coronavirus is producing a number of destructive physical and material results in our global world. It is undercutting economic growth and public health. It has put people out of work and changed our lifestyles. Countless individuals have been hospitalized; thousands have died. Its physical impact is undeniable. We will not be the same post COVID-19. For many, the impact has been a real threat to the first hunger—sustaining physical health and personal well-being.

At the same time, COVID-19 has had an impact on our spiritual hunger as well. In the midst of this virus, we've been asked to keep our social distance and stay close to home. During this time, I have noticed something significant and palpable taking place in my neighborhood. It can be witnessed physically, but it has more than simple material value. It involves the spiritual realm before it is expressed physically. Ironically, it is clearly noticed when it is absent.

During these months, I saw neighbors stop to talk with each other in the street (at a safe physical distance, of course), when previously this seldom happened. I saw parents playing basketball or biking with their kids. I saw sidewalk chalk pictures and people working in their yards and visiting with each other as neighbors passed by. I saw casual acquaintances offer to help out neighbors, when such offers seldom happened previously.

Somehow this deadly virus, which was attacking our first hunger of physical well-being, was simultaneously feeding our second hunger for meaning and connection with each other. It is ironic that the coronavirus, which is traveling on an invisible level and creating physical distance between us, and our spiritual "better angels," which also travel in an invisible way, have converged in real time. The result: this deadly virus has put us in closer proximity to each other spiritually, even as it requires us to be further apart physically. This is not to diminish the destructive consequences of the coronavirus, but it is to say that if these spiritual practices are sustained, our social connections with each other might improve for the better.

During times such as this, some will reach out to others, while others will buy guns, some will decide to volunteer to help those in need, while others will hoard essentials. These physical actions are the result of the prior activity taking place within.

Why is it that physical distress and disaster so often feed our deep hungers just when our physical hunger is at greatest risk? Think hurricane, earthquake, and flood here. Why does spiritual connection take place and release our "better angels" at precisely the moment when we are in the greatest physical/material danger? Perhaps it is that during such times we see each other as fellow human beings most clearly.

Today, we are at a critical crossroads regarding our spiritual well-being. Our future, individually and collectively, is hanging in the balance. Jacob Needleman states it well in his book, *The American Soul*:

> It is hard to resist seeing the state of the nation as a mirror of our own inner condition. And it is only one step from this comparison to the idea that society always and everywhere is what it is solely because individual human beings are what they are.[3]

What we see politically and socially in our world is simply a reflection of our collective inner spirits.

We've heard a lot of talk in recent years about "making America great again," but the focus of this quest has been on a false sense of greatness that is measured in physical terms that concentrates on wealth, power, and material success. It depicts an artificial greatness that assumes goodness without considering the faults and blemishes that also mark our history.

True greatness is about much more than this and is measured in spiritual terms, which include matters of compassion, love, justice, peace, and community.

True greatness can't occur without there being a significant level of self-reflection and inner searching taking place that has to do with identity and meaning. Spiritual greatness is not something that any person or society does in isolation. This kind of greatness is forged in the struggles and realities of community life from marriage and parenthood to being a neighbor and citizen.

These dynamics aren't being given adequate consideration in our nation's current search for greatness. Instead, we have become satisfied with seeking lesser, more narrowly defined goals that have to do with materiality. We are doing this at our own collective detriment.

Greatness literally requires something more from us that we have ignored: visiting unpleasant experiences, identifying personal and collective weaknesses and vulnerabilities, moving toward hope and goodness rather

---

3. Needleman, *American Soul*, 124.

than despair and mean-spiritedness. Greatness has to do with reaching new heights within our character, not having more material goods than our neighbors. Greatness is something worth setting our sights on, but only by way of a humble, self-reflective path. This journey will not be easy, but it is time to begin.

John Cage's words "Begin anywhere"[4] appear prominently on my desk at home as a reminder that one doesn't need to have an elaborate plan nor a meticulous schedule in place in order to live a spiritually grounded life. That would be a "New Year's Resolution" approach to spiritual life that more often than not fails miserably. Such an approach may work for a few weeks or months, but eventually this "crash course" approach does exactly that—crash. Spirituality needs to be integrated into how one sees and experiences everything in life, all the time. And you can begin anywhere!

I encourage you to ponder these pages and integrate the material found here into your inner-being. It begins by simply looking around in new ways. The first step can happen anywhere. Once you start to do this work somewhere, you will soon find yourself living a spiritually grounded way of life everywhere!

In many ways, it is not unlike working on a giant puzzle. There are times when it is impossible to see how all the pieces will fit together, and then suddenly one or two pieces make sense and a whole section of the puzzle comes together, even though other parts still remain a mystery. In the spiritual realm, it is difficult to see everything all at once. We get inklings here and there as things come together. Some things will remain unclear, perhaps even to the very end.

This is how the spirit works when it comes alive. Sometimes spirituality happens in big spurts, but more often than not it happens in small, but profound, ways. It is why Brother Lawrence, the humble seventeenth-century mystic, could find himself in God's presence even while washing dishes. Spirituality, by its very nature, stops the normal flow of life's activity and grounds you in the present. Once experienced, spirituality is contagious, so it changes what is going on within the larger community, as well.

In this journey, it is important to remember that spirituality and religion are not the same thing. While religion can be a source of spiritual life for many, it can also be a barrier. Brené Brown expresses this difference well when she says, "I bolted from organized religion when it got too

---

4. Popular saying attributed to the American composer, John Cage (1912–92).

hard to find God—when politics and certainty replaced mystery and faith."[5] Religion can be either the source or a barrier to experiencing mystery and faith in life. It all depends on whether it turns a person out into the world in freeing, life-giving ways or it turns one into an overly pious person who is filled with a sense of certainty and judgement.

When the spirit becomes a vital part of our world, we pay attention to things and people differently. Perhaps this is why so many of the great spiritual teachers focused their teachings on developing spiritual awareness, staying alert, and being fully awake as the first step in living a spiritual life. Without doing these things, all one sees is the material world. That way of seeing misses what matters most, including what the Christian Apostle Paul called the "fruit of the spirit": love, joy, peace, forbearance, kindness, goodness, faithfulness, gentleness, and self-control (Gal 5:22–23).

This book is divided into three parts. Part I is about the inner life. It deals with how one's understanding moves in an inward-out direction and how we can focus on those spiritual qualities that are worth measuring. Part II focuses on four particular qualities that lead to spiritual wholeness. They are finding center, framing, practicing, and living with others. Finally, Part III outlines both universal and uniquely American barriers to becoming spiritually grounded and socially responsible. This section concludes with chapters on dealing with conflict and discovering one's life calling since these two factors play an important role in overcoming our current state of affairs. In order to move forward in a positive way, we will need to be intentional and disciplined, but also be mindful of the opportunities and signs of spiritual life around us. We will need to pay attention differently and set down old, ineffective ways.

In his book, *Coincidence or Destiny? Stories of Synchronicity that Illuminate Our Lives*, Phil Cousineau writes:

> The challenge will be to know what is trivial and what is meaningful, what is grandiose and what is genuine, in these maverick experiences called synchronicity. Suffice it to say they are more than chance, less than causality; more than magic, less than fantasy. More an enigmatic pattern suddenly detected, than a solid link in a chain finally proved.[6]

Life isn't an accident; it has purpose and meaning. It is up to us to notice the possibilities of each moment for this to be so. I invite you to join me on the

5. Brown, "6 favorite books," line 26.

6. Cousineau, *Coincidence or Destiny?*, 278.

adventure ahead and see the world through a spiritual lens. It will change your life . . . and it may very well determine if we will successfully heal our nation in the coming days.

Lowell Greathouse
Spring 2020

PART I

The Journey Begins Within

WE LIVE AT A critical moment in American history in which the symbiotic relationship and the give-and-take that occurs between spirituality and politics are on full display. On one level, this should not be surprising. There is always an interplay between the personal and the social dimensions of life.

Today it takes the form of people, moved by the spirit, going to the streets to protest against racial injustice and oppression, essential workers risking their lives to provide the basic services we need in order to have a functioning society, and incredible moments in which, in the midst of stress and tension, individuals open their hearts to touch the lives of others in powerful and lasting ways. These personal actions come from within, and as they become concrete action, they speak eloquently about the nature of the human spirit and its ability to have a social impact.

Throughout history, from the ancient Greeks and Hebrews to those of us living in contemporary America, societies have wrestled with the fundamental qualities of the personal-social dynamic. Each era has documented this grappling, including ancient political/ philosophical writings, the Judeo-Christian heritage of the Ten Commandments, and in more contemporary settings through everything from congressional hearings to curb immoral/unethical behavior within the political realm to political protests against injustice and structural inequality.

The Ten Commandments, which were written by the ancient Hebrews, framed political life in deeply religious terms that reflected both a personal and a social quality. They represent a classic example of a society codifying socio-personal and material/spiritual relationships in order to define its parameters. Here was a social order that understood that if an individual's behaviors involved coveting a neighbor's spouse, lying to others, or committing violence against someone, that these behaviors not only reflected a person's own moral decay but also produced negative social ramifications in the larger community.

The later definition of the "Seven Deadly Sins" within the Christian tradition is yet another example of a spiritual community grappling with the symbiosis between the personal and the social, the spiritual and the political realms of life.

These imbalances were called the "Seven Deadly Sins," because they were seen as going against fundamental spiritual values. They have a long history within the Christian tradition and date back to the sixth century, when they were first enumerated. They gained greater prominence in the thirteenth century when Thomas Aquinas elaborated on their meaning within Christianity.

These classic sins were described as pride, greed, lust, envy, gluttony, wrath, and sloth. Each one was seen as damaging the human spirit when not attended to in healthy, whole ways in both personal and social relationships.

Interestingly, each of these sins isn't really about the material world, but first and foremost about our inability to address matters within our spirits. As we will discuss throughout this book, our individual spiritual lives do not take place in isolation; they always produce ramifications within a larger social setting.

Our current culture markets many of the traits associated with the Seven Deadly Sins in positive terms, hoping to encourage certain behaviors that will produce financial or material benefit for those seeking to take advantage of others (e.g., "What happens in Vegas, stays in Vegas"). This is predicated on the notion that someone will gain from another person's weakness, vulnerability, misfortune, or pain. When this happens, there is a spiritual dissonance that occurs in society that results in personal and social dysfunction for the purpose of someone's economic and material gain. Gambling, payday lending, and prostitution are good examples of this phenomenon.

In the twentieth century, Mohandas Gandhi and others looked at these personal traits through a larger social lens. In 1925, Gandhi printed a list of Seven Social Sins that he believed society needed to address in order for it to be healthy and whole. Those sins are politics without principles, wealth without work, pleasure without conscience, business without ethics, knowledge without character, science without humanity, and religion without sacrifice.[1]

Much like the earlier Christian list of deadly sins, this list of social sins is an expression of the interplay between the personal and the social, moving in an inside-out manner. If we work collectively, we are capable of creating positive growth and balance in our personal lives as well.

These are not small nor insignificant issues. They appear at the heart of our identity. They intersect with each other and determine who we are as individuals and as a society.

The formation of the American experiment in the late 1790s is yet another example of a society trying to come to terms with how to live as a community while honoring individual difference and seeking collective harmony. Jacob Needleman points this out in his writings:

> The originators of America were not mystics; not monks, not contemplatives. But neither were the most dynamic of them mere materialists, exploiters or cunning businessmen. America was the creation of a collection of men in whom traces of ancient interior spiritual truths were honored alongside the need to organize an immense new world of phenomenal potential wealth and power. This simultaneity of the spiritual and material was of quite new coloration and energy. This simultaneity was America.[2]

It is this unique social experiment that is at risk today, precisely because we have ignored the attacks taking place on our spiritual well-being for too long, falsely assuming that today's concerns are only political in nature. Nothing could be further from the truth.

The spiritual toxins that plague us today are significant. When they enter our collective national bloodstream, they make their way to the heart and soul of our nation and cause severe damage. The classic "deadly sins" of pride, greed, lust, anger, gluttony, envy, and sloth have been a problem that individuals and societies have faced since the beginning of time, but there are other toxins which we face today that have compounded the issue.

Today, because of social media and the 24/7 ability to communicate, our inner spirits are flooded with information and stories, tweets and visual images that impact both our individual and collective consciousness.

---

1. Mohandas Gandhi published the list of the Seven Social Sins in his weekly newspaper *Young India* on October 22, 1925. They were first uttered in a sermon at Westminster Abbey on March 20, 1925 by Rev. Frederick Lewis Donaldson.

2. Needleman, *American Soul*, 125.

From social media aggression to unaddressed white privilege, from the degradation of sexuality to the excessive focus on celebrity, wealth, and power, we have increased the complexities we face spiritually as we try to find an appropriate way forward to maintain a civil, harmonious society.

Life moves in an inward-out manner. Our interior, personal lives work themselves out through our social realities, but are also impacted by those larger realities at the same time. This dance goes on-and-on, back and forth. One learns the art of giving by understanding what it means to receive. Hostility turns to hospitality through deep, inner work, as does the movement from hate to love.

Martin Luther King Jr. put it well when he said, "Darkness cannot drive out darkness; only light can do that. Hate cannot drive out hate; only love can do that."[3] This is true because spirituality foreshadows and interacts with politics. The fundamental battles regarding good and evil take place first within the human soul.

We have, at our disposal, thousands of outstanding spiritual resources available to us from a variety of traditions and cultures. They mark the ancient, but universal, longings of the human heart. Yet, because of the choices we are making as individuals and as a society, we still have not figured out how to utilize these resources in ways that can successfully guide us through our current social problems.

Instead, in recent years, we have increasingly become more interested in seeking out agreement, similarity, and common identity politically rather than exploring the vastness and diversity of creation and the larger, global community we are a part of with a sense of openness and curiosity. The result is that we have become spiritually diminished as individuals and as a society, while becoming more politically divided.

These dynamics have been a part of our cultural life for some time, perhaps even going back to the very beginning of the American experiment. But this reality has become especially pronounced in recent years.

Interestingly, early signs of this struggle appeared in a 1970s speech, when President Jimmy Carter famously spoke about what commentators quickly coined as his "malaise speech." In that speech, Carter expressed his concern about " . . . a crisis that strikes at the very heart and soul and spirit of our national will. We can see this crisis in the growing doubt about the meaning of our own lives and in the loss of a unity of purpose for our nation."[4]

3. King, *Strength to Love*, 51.

4. From President Jimmy Carter's speech televised nationally on July 14, 1979.

Rather than explore and confront what this meant at a deeper national level, our country moved on to President Reagan's "It's Morning in America Again" approach to national identity, which emphasized wealth, prosperity, and power over reflection, conversation, and harmony. The hard spiritual, ethical questions that are still with us today were put aside as material success and economic prosperity took center stage.

Time has passed, but the deep political divisions and spiritual disunity we see so clearly growing among us today have been with us for over forty years. Their impact is significant and chronic, even as American presidents from Reagan to Trump have tried to address it in a variety of ineffective and misguided ways. Each effort has neglected to address our growing spiritual bankruptcy.

It is one thing to set up a White House Office of Faith-Based and Neighborhood Partnerships, as President George W. Bush did during his administration, but it is something quite different to create public space for spiritual reflection to become a part of our social life and expression. In short, one is about religious-political institutional possibilities and boundaries within a separation of church and state constitutional republic model. The other is about creating latitude for the natural flow between the material and the spiritual to be acknowledged as a part of our social framework.

The former runs the risk of codifying church/state relationships, while the latter is about embracing the world with openness and value qualities such as compassion, justice, and love, as well as material wealth and economic success.

There is little to dispute the reality that we lack healthy wholeness as a country, even as we appear to have gained a greater sense of national self-certainty toward the rest of the world. Perhaps this has occurred because we are simply not self-reflective or self-disciplined enough to make the important connections between the material and spiritual worlds.

Deep, spiritual work is not easy. It takes time and energy, and it requires a willingness to be self-discerning and open to those around us who see things in different ways. It means constructive conversations that include listening as well as talking. In short, while we have been appropriately alarmed at the melting of the polar ice caps and the problem of climate change, we have failed to pay attention to the simultaneous inner climate change and soul melting going on in our hearts. The result is the very real danger that spiritual degradation will continue to be a part of our future. If our spirits are damaged in this way, it will be nearly impossible to find our way forward socially and politically.

Robert Bellah, in his work, *The Good Society*, frames things in this way:

> The great classic criteria of a good society—peace, prosperity, freedom, justice—all depend today on a new experiment in democracy, a newly extended set of democratic institutions, within which citizens can better discern what we really want and what we ought to want to sustain a good life on this planet for ourselves and the generations to come.[5]

In the absence of focusing on spiritual matters, the United States now finds itself in a morass in which we are politically stuck and spiritually bankrupt.

Perhaps we are in a similar situation that Scrooge found himself in at the end of Charles Dickens' wonderful work, *The Christmas Carol*. Once he discovered the realities that surrounded him, Scrooge had a dramatic change of heart. But as big of a challenge as this awareness was for him, the greater challenge was to change his ways, not just for Christmas, but throughout the year. As Scrooge says at the end of the story, "I will honor Christmas in my heart, and try to keep it all the year."[6]

Today we face a comparable challenge: Can we not only see and understand the spiritual realities around us, but will that awareness change who we are throughout the year?

5. Bellah, *Good Society*, 9.

6. Dickens, *Christmas Carol*. First published December 1843.

1

Measuring What We Are Really Worth

Spiritual Principles and Moral Markers

IN ORDER TO FIND our way spiritually, we will need to cultivate an ability to understand life in spiritual terms. This doesn't mean attending church, mosque, or synagogue more often nor in saying prayers more regularly. Finding our way spiritually has to do with seeing life through a spiritual lens and by using tools such as compassion, awe, and love to guide us in the ways we relate to our surroundings.

Spiritual markers focus our attention on a variety of principles that serve both as tools and measures for seeing and experiencing the world differently. When we practice these principles as individuals, society changes, and when we collectively embody them, we see the world differently.

This means that we each have an important role to play in our unfolding future as a people. If we are to find our way out of our current dysfunctional situation, we will all need to embrace a more spiritual understanding of life on some level, even as we seek out political and social leadership to help guide us along the way.

Marianne Williamson, in her book, *The Healing of America*, put it this way back in 1997:

> We are organized in the United States today according to obsolete social principles, obsolete because they reflect separation from spirit. They posit us as purely material rather than spiritual beings, and economically oriented rather than relationship-oriented people.[1]

1. Williamson, *Healing of America*, 25.

Not much has changed since Williamson wrote these words. If anything, matters have only gotten worse.

It is past time to reframe our national landscape so that we think and act differently toward ourselves and one another. This book is an invitation into that conversation. We need to use the rich, spiritual resources at our disposal to move in new, more productive directions and remember and regain a sense of our common humanity.

This is a tall order, especially since there are signs all around that indicate our spiritual lives are out of order. The essence of our personal and social being is at stake, and we aren't addressing it with any sense of urgency or commitment. We are not attending to the spiritual basics that can guide us out of our current state of affairs and move us forward.

As Americans, we love to measure things—everything. We look at outcomes and indicators, goals and strategies, vision statements and New Year's Resolutions. How are we doing? How can we get better? Are we great? Will we break new records?

We have plenty of measures that indicate when we are doing well materially, from stock markets that have reached record heights to statistics that represent historically low levels of unemployment in our country. Yet in spite of this, it is easy to see that we are in deep trouble spiritually, even though these measures don't make the headlines of our newspapers.

Yes, the rich are getting richer. Yes, the number of millionaires in the United States has hit an all-time high. Yes, the United States has the world's highest Gross Domestic Product (GDP).

But there are other ways to measure how things are going in the United States that have more to do with spiritual matters. Consider these measures:

- The United States has dropped to 19th among 156 nations ranked in the World Happiness Report (2019). This annual report is a product of the United Nations Sustainable Development Solutions Network. It measures fourteen different key social factors, including health, safety, education, and emotional well-being, in terms of a society's sense of happiness. The 2019 ranking represents the US's lowest rating ever.[2]

  What does it mean to be materially #1, but #19 in terms of social happiness?

---

2. Helliwell et al., *World Happiness Report.*

- Hate crimes continue to be recorded at heightened levels in recent years, and this is clearly a national problem.[3]

  What does it mean for a society to have widespread violence perpetrated against people of different races and cultures?

- Charitable giving has continued to decrease in the US since 2000 and, thanks in large part to the new 2017 Tax Reform changes, this decrease will likely continue in the future.[4]

  What does it mean to have a lesser commitment to giving to others as a society?

- There were 434 mass shootings in the US in 2019 or 1.19 per day. This number far exceeds any other country in the world.[5]

  Why is mass violence such a common occurrence in a nation as wealthy as ours?

- The gap between the rich and poor in the country continues to widen annually.[6]

  What does it mean that some people have much more than they need, while others simply try make ends meet on a daily basis, adding stress, anxiety, and uncertainty to their lives?

One can clearly see our spiritual dysfunction exposed through our lack of civility in the public arena and in the growth of hatred, bigotry, and violence among us. In social media, individuals experience bullying in damaging ways. People weaponize the use of their cars, making our public roads places of hostility. Our government talks more about constructing walls and arming ourselves, both physically, militarily, and economically, than it does about building bridges of understanding between us. The signs of social and spiritual unrest are evident everywhere.

When you listen to the news each week, you can see all of the Seven Deadly Sins—pride, greed, lust, anger, gluttony, envy, and sloth—displayed

---

3. McCarthy, "U.S. Hate Crimes"; and US Department of Justice, *2018 Hate Crime Statistics*.

4. "Americans gave $427.71 billion to charity in 2018 amid complex year for charitable giving," *Giving USA*.

5. "US mass killings hit a record high in 2019," *USA Today*.

6. Fadulu, "Study Shows Income Gap Between Rich and Poor Keeps Growing, with Deadly Effects."

on a regular basis. Many have even weaponized their places of worship, making it difficult to gather in the spirit of humbleness and community, even in settings in which we have come together historically in order to find meaning and connect with transcendent reality.

One can tell what matters most in a society by what people discuss and in the topics of conversation. Another measure is reflected in what we see on television, in the movies, and by what appears on social media and through tweets.

If this is the case, we may be in more trouble than we think. Our media is filled with excessive violence and gratuitous sex, hate-filled language and vicious bullying. Media is often seen as a form of entertainment, so what is so entertaining about these things? Sometimes it is difficult to decide whether the media depicts or determines the qualities of our society.

Where we find ourselves as a society isn't the result of some nameless, faceless force overtaking us. It is about us, as human beings and citizens, losing our spiritual compass and wandering down paths that destroy our social fabric and damage our relationships with one another. Taken together, these dynamics have resulted in the squandering of our collective resources for social good.

Quite frankly, in our quest for greatness, we've been focusing our attention on the wrong things. As a result, we've not measured what truly matters. Robert Kennedy said it best back in 1968:

> [Our] GNP—if we should judge America by that—counts air pollution and cigarette advertising, and ambulances to clear our highways of carnage. It counts special locks for our doors and the jails for those who break them. It counts the destruction of our redwoods—and the loss of our natural wonder in the chaotic sprawl. It counts napalm and the cost of a nuclear warhead, and armored cars for police who fight riots in our streets. It counts . . . the television programs which glorify violence in order to sell toys to our children.
>
> Yet the gross national product does not allow for the health of our children, the quality of their education, or the joy of their play. It does not include the beauty of our poetry or the strength of our marriages, the intelligence of our public debate or the integrity of our public officials. It measures neither our wit nor our courage; neither our wisdom nor our learning; neither our compassion nor our devotion to our country; it measures everything, in short, except that which makes life worthwhile . . .[7]

7. MacAfee, *Gospel According to RFK*, 41. This speech was given by Senator Robert F.

Perhaps we haven't been measuring the things that matter most. But, is it even possible to live in a monopolistic capitalist society and have a spiritual life? Or have we created such a dramatic imbalance between the material and spiritual, by expanding our sense of capitalism far beyond what the economist Adam Smith and others originally intended when they advocated for it, that we can no longer live whole, healthy lives?

Robert Kuttner addresses this question by reminding us that capitalism wasn't just about profit margins and material welling being:

> Smith promoted free markets as a source of competition against royal monopolies. But he supported a society of mutual obligation, warned against private monopolies and the tendency of owners to take advantage of workers, and was a strong backer of public investment in education.[8]

Following the height of the Gilded Age in the early 1900s, when a few at the top of the economic ladder possessed remarkable wealth and power, Andrew Carnegie spoke out about people of wealth, even though he was one of them. He said that those who passed their excess wealth onto their families at the end of their lives rather than give it to the community for social good were people of disgrace rather than honor. They simply weren't aware of nor understood their wealth in terms of community connection.

David Nasaw says as much in his introduction to Andrew Carnegie's essay "Gospel of Wealth":

> Carnegie scorned those who left their fortunes to their children. To provide children with more than a moderate income was to ruin them. It was thus the duty of the rich man to give away all he had while he was alive. If, through sloth or avarice, the rich did not give away their fortunes, it was incumbent on government to do so after their deaths. Carnegie supported a nearly 100 percent estate tax because he believed it provided an incentive for the rich to dispose of their fortunes during their lifetimes.[9]

This is a far cry from our current laws that continue to support generational wealth accumulation. Interestingly, Carnegie's understanding of the role of material possessions in relationship to a person's soul was closer to Jesus'

Kennedy at University of Kansas, March 18, 1968.

8. Kuttner, "Blaming Liberalism," 38.

9. Carnegie, *"Gospel of Wealth" Essays and Other Writings*, xi.

teaching "What good is it for someone to gain the whole world, yet forfeit their soul" (Mark 8:36)? than it is to current American laws and practices.

There are clear spiritual signs that indicate that all is not well with our souls. One easy, but ancient, way to assess our situation and measure it would be to use the Apostle Paul's first-century criteria of assessing what he called "the fruit of the spirit," which includes love, joy, peace, forbearance, kindness, goodness, faithfulness, gentleness, and self-control (Gal 5:22–23). A simple spiritual assessment could involve these questions:

- When you look at your own life, the interactions in your family, at work, in your neighborhood, and in our nation, how do you think we are doing in terms of the "fruit of the spirit" today?

- Do you experience patience while driving to work?

- Do you see kindness, love, and joy displayed in the settings listed above?

- Do our political leaders demonstrate goodness and self-control?

- Is there peace and a feeling of gentleness between us as neighbors?

- Are we being faithful to living out our spiritual beliefs?

As much attention as there has been on the threat of climate change in our world, little attention has been paid to the spiritual changes that continue to damage what Carl Jung referred to as the "collective unconscious" (i.e., the amalgamation of shaped ideas across humanity). Quite literally, our spiritual firmament has been badly impaired by recent human activity and the pollution that has resulted from our actions is now impacting our concepts of awe, blessing, and wonder among other things. We are facing a significant climate change in our spiritual world at the same time we are experiencing a devastating climate change in the physical world. It is not farfetched to say that the two are integrally related.

In order to correct this, the first step is to assess how we are doing in terms of spiritual qualities such as kindness, love, gentleness, etc. These qualities are spiritual practices, as well as indicators of spiritual well-being.

If we don't develop better civic practices and learn how to improve our spiritual progress, we will continue to measure our health, success, and greatness in material terms alone. This will not help us understand how we are doing as a people nor point us in the direction of wholeness and harmony, which are among the key measures of spiritual progress.

For Further Study and Reflection

- What words best describe your sense of success? How are you doing in these areas? What changes would you make?

- From Paul's list of "fruit of the Spirit," which ones would you use to describe yourself?

- What words do you think others use to describe who you are as a person? What is your reaction to these markers of your character?

2

An Inward-Out Movement

If there is to be peace in the nations, there must be peace in the cities.
If there is to be peace in the cities, there must be peace between neighbors.
If there is to be peace between neighbors, there must be peace in the home.
If there is to be peace in the home, there must be peace in the heart.

—AUTHOR UNKNOWN[1]

LIFE IS AN INWARD-OUT journey. Our attitudes shape how we see and act in the world. Thought proceeds action. The heart pumps the life blood that activates our hands and feet. We are beings before we are doings.

Let me illustrate it in the way. Consider our attitudes and behaviors related to driving. When we drive in a car, there is a significant difference between thinking in terms of "driving defensively" and having the opinion that "all other drivers are morons."

The former expression is wise counsel and reflects an interactive understanding that everyone should drive defensively in order for the highways to be safe. Accidents can happen as a result of someone's carelessness.

The latter expression that "all other drivers are morons" is a strong judgement about other people that is negative, hostile, and diminishes social relationships on our streets and highways. It holds a pejorative opinion of fellow travelers, whether or not an accident ever occurs. It assumes that

1. Author unknown, though it is often credited to Lao Tzu in the *Tao te ching*. It most closely relates to entry #54. See Le Guin, *Lao Tzu*, 79.

others are stupid and irresponsible. If anything happens, it is somebody else's fault. This opinion undercuts the spiritual connection between people we don't even know: You are a moron, we think, even before anything happens. At the same time, it eliminates the element of self-reflection from our examination of driving. Is it possible that I could cause an accident myself? Probably not if everyone else is a moron to begin with!

Both viewpoints germinate first as personal, inner feelings toward others, framing our view of fellow travelers, reinforcing our attitudes and behaviors, and ultimately determining how we engage and interact with others on the road.

If they, like us, need to be aware and cautious when driving, then we are on the journey together, and we will all pay attention to each other in order to avoid accidents. But if everyone else is a "moron," just waiting to do something wrong, then this presumes that I am superior. When a mistake is made it is someone else's fault. Why not flip them off or yell at them when driving as ways to demonstrate my offense at their stupidity? After all, they are idiots to begin with!

What we say to ourselves within precedes what we do through our actions and behaviors. This simple example reflects just one of the many ways in which we operationalize our inner attitudes toward others. It is an inward-out movement that has spiritual and social ramifications. Our perspectives eventually have social implications that impact community life.

This type of hostile viewpoint is also reflected in the dismissive way in which many people view and treat government. Think for a moment: Is your attitude toward government spiritually grounded, believing that, because power and ambition corrupt, we need checks and balances in place within society, but that people in government are genuinely interested in serving the public? Or do you just distrust all government activity, assuming that everyone associated with public service is corrupt, against social progress, and responsible for evil?

One attitude moves us toward social connection, while the other creates a natural feeling of division, contempt, and hostility, viewing some people as inferior. In its extreme forms, one attitude led to the bombing of the Federal Building in Oklahoma City, while for others the Peace Corps became the kind of government program that brought out the highest aspirations of many young people who served our country in countless places across the globe. On a more basic level, our inner attitudes toward those in government relate to everything from the microaggressions that people express toward those in public service to expressions such as "good enough for government work."

The perspectives that reflect our inner voice find expression in how we treat others. These inward-out attitudes repeat themselves in many forms on a daily basis. In the end, they dictate the social environment that we create among us.

Today, our spiritual development appears to be stunted in a number of significant ways, including the two examples highlighted above. Because of this, now is the time for us to revisit ancient spiritual teachings and find contemporary ways to express them so we can integrate this wisdom into our lives in ways that will save us from our current political chaos and spiritual dementia. Inward-out living requires self-reflection, which includes taking time to examine what we think and believe before we act. There is no peace anywhere until there is peace within.

The movie *Inside Out*, by Pixar, is a wonderful example of what the inward-out spiritual movement actually entails. In this movie we see a variety of voices and emotions competing for attention and control inside Riley, the little girl who is the main character in the film. What Riley experiences is true of our lives as well. Those feelings and emotions that are given voice inside us try to take control and determine what we will do and ultimately who we are in a given situation.

This dynamic should not be unfamiliar to those of us who are aware of the great spiritual traditions. There are many internal voices competing all the time for our attention. The spiritual question is: What voice, among the many inner voices, do we respond to? Which one is most spiritually grounded, so that our actions reflect who we are and want to be?

Howard Thurman, the great twentieth-century spiritual guide, put it this way:

> We are all of us deeply involved in the throes of our own weaknesses and strengths, expressed often in the profoundest conflicts within our own souls. The only hope for surcease, the only possibility of stability for the person, is to establish an Island of Peace within one's own soul. Here one brings for review the purposes and dreams to which one's life is tied . . . Well within the island is the Temple where God dwells—not the God of creed, the church, the family, but the God of one's heart.[2]

This is what it means to live in a heartfelt, inward-out way.

2. Thurman, *Meditations of the Heart*, 17

16

When the inward-out movement becomes a natural spiritual flow within one's life, the merger between the material world and spiritual reality becomes incarnational in nature (i.e., a living being who embodies divine spirit). This doesn't turn one into a god by any means, but when an individual lives in this way—inward-out—those traits that we believe are divine or godly become visible in real time through a person's life.

It isn't just a matter of doing nice things; it is about becoming kindness. It isn't about saying thank you to someone; it is about being filled with gratitude. It isn't about proclaiming you understand how someone feels when they are poorly treated; it is about embodying justice.

It is similar to what happens when a musician simply becomes the music they are playing or a performer becomes the character they are embodying. When this happens in our daily lives in a profound, inward-out manner, these times become holy moments, even though they are frequently fleeting within our lives.

This is why Jesus represents divinity in the Christian experience or Mohandas Gandhi and others are considered holy teachers within other traditions. When we witness their actions publicly—moving in an inward-out motion—they represent what we believe it would be like if God were present in the situation. They reflect a unified human being, who is able to find, listen to, and embody their "better angels."

Perhaps this is why we are so deeply moved when we see a Good Samaritan coming to the aid of a stranger, or a police officer kneeling with a protester, or an individual risking their life on behalf of someone who is vulnerable or in danger. These inner-inspired actions find residence within our own souls and suddenly something that is fixed in time (i.e., that is momentary), becomes something that transcends time (i.e., becomes lasting), and we are changed by what we see with our eyes and feel with our hearts.

For Further Study and Reflection

- Who is someone you know or have read about who lived in an inside-out manner? What is it about their behavior that you admire?

- Take a moment to visualize an altar at the center of your being. What do you see there? What and who have you allowed to dwell there?

- We all have voices within that compete for our attention. How would you name the voices inside you that beckon for your attention? Which ones need to be given voice? Which ones need to be ignored?

PART II

Four Qualities of Spiritual Wholeness

ALL THE TIME, BOTH individually and collectively, we make value choices that impact how we see each other as human beings and determine what kind of society we decide to live in. The result of these choices within the United States is that we have created what could be called a predominantly "marketplace culture," which values people and things in a strictly economic, material manner. This marketplace culture mediates the ways we function, shapes how we view others, and determines what and who we pay attention to.

The great contradiction of our time is that while our phones and technologies tell us exactly where we are physically, we appear to be totally lost spiritually. It is time to pause long enough to read the signs of the times so we can make progress collectively and become healthier spiritually. Frederic and Mary Ann Brussat say we must develop a sense of spiritual literacy, which would give us " . . . the ability to read the signs written in the texts of our own experiences."[1]

Thoughtful public thinkers address these matters, as has been with case with Jon Meacham's *The Soul of America*, Robert Bellah's *Habits of the Heart*, Robert Putnam's *Bowling Alone* and *Better Together*, and others. To date, however, we tend to focus more of our attention on the political dimensions of our current crisis without fully grasping its prior, deep spiritual significance.

For the most part, we have failed to see spirituality as being at the heart of our collective struggles. If we continue on this path, we do so at our

---

1. Brussat and Brussat, *Spiritual Literacy*, 15.

own individual and collective peril. This approach will not move us from political brokenness to spiritual wholeness.

In their book, *Metaphors We Live By*, George Lakoff and Mark Johnson, describe how the conceptual frameworks we create for ourselves share and influence the realities we live in:

> The concepts that govern our thought are not just matters of the intellect. They also govern our everyday functioning, down to the most mundane details. Our concepts structure what we perceive, how we get around in the world, and how we relate to other people. Our conceptual system thus plays a central role in defining our everyday realities. If we are right in suggesting that our conceptual system is largely metaphorical, then the way we think, what we experience, and what we do every day is very much a matter of metaphor.[2]

We have been living with metaphorical imagery that leads to conflict, division, and hostility for some time. We need to change directions and seek common spiritual ground if we are to survive as a nation and as a world. I am hopeful that we are capable of doing this. In fact, Lakoff and Johnson go on to say, "New metaphors are capable of creating new understandings and, therefore, new realities."[3] We can do this. The question is: Will we decide to make the changes needed in order to preserve our collective future? The outcome is up to us.

We desperately need to determine how to go to the source of our difficulties, which lie within the human spirit itself, so we can come to terms with what it means to live life in the twenty-first century.

In different spiritual traditions, the quest for inner peace and social harmony is depicted as an ascent of a great mountain. It is easy to see why this would be the case. Such a journey involves an adventure that includes focus, clarity of purpose, skill and determination, and teamwork with others. It is not something that one undertakes alone nor is it done without adequate preparation or the gathering of appropriate training and supplies.

In the exploration of the four qualities of spiritual wholeness, I am inviting you to join me on a quest to understand those traits that are needed to successfully ascend to the highest summits of life.

In order to free the inward-out movement of the spirit so it can be anchored in our lives, there are four personal and social qualities that need to be cultivated and developed. These qualities are (1) Centering—Grounding

2. Lakoff and Johnson, *Metaphors We Live By*, 3.
3. Lakoff and Johnson, *Metaphors We Live By*, 235.

and Seeing Reality with Clarity; (2) Framing—Making Sense of the World; (3) Practicing—Turning Spiritual Principles into Personal Habits; and (4) Living with Others—Engaging Life with Wholeness.

In a way, they represent fundamental, primal qualities that are central to life itself, much like some indigenous cultures identified earth, fire, wind, and water as primary elements in earlier times. One could even see these four spiritual qualities as representing the breath of life itself. The first two—centering and framing—embody a kind of inhaling spiritually, so that we are anchored and able to engage the world. The second two—practicing and living with others—represent a spiritual exhale, in which we interact with those around us. Literally, breathing our inner lives onto each other. Together, these four qualities represent our very breath and life force.

It could be said that these four spiritual elements serve as a *yin* and *yang* of sorts, reflecting both the inward-out movement of the spirit when it is fully at work, as well as the give and take that is in constant motion between the spiritual and the material, the personal and the social. We will look at each of these characteristics separately to see why they collectively are so important in our journey to recover the spirit in times of political brokenness.

However, it is important to note that while some individuals will be able to easily practice these principles through their current religious traditions, others will need to develop their own approach to incorporating these qualities into their lives through personal study or find ways to enhance the basic spiritual foundation they receive through their religious customs.

Not all religious institutions have maintained a sense of active vitality regarding these four characteristics. Those who have a deep desire for spiritual wakefulness outside of a particular religious tradition may need to become more intentional regarding these traits. In any case, we will not make progress individually or collectively if we are not able to ground our lives in centering, framing, practicing, and living with others in ways that move us toward spiritual health and wholeness.

3

Centering

Grounding and Seeing Reality with Clarity

As long as there is light in one's heart, you can always find home.

—RUMI[1]

SPIRITUALITY IS ABOUT MOUNTAIN-TOP experiences and deep dives into our inner lives. As we begin the spiritual journey, it is important to be prepared and ready to make the climb. In many ways, creating an appropriate base camp is an essential first step. Until we have done that, it is difficult to know what kind of journey we have undertaken, if we have the supplies we need, or whether we even know where we are headed. Is this just a simple stroll in the park or have we undertaken something of greater significance? If this is a major climb to an unknown summit, then we had better prepare ourselves appropriately.

Do we have the supplies we need? Have we properly researched what will be involved in the climb? While there are many routes to the summit, do we know which path we will start out using? Because there will be unexpected challenges along the way, are we aware of the resources we may need to utilize? Do we know how to contact others if we need assistance? Do we

---

1. This is a popular quote widely attributed to Rumi, a thirteenth-century Persian poet and Islamic scholar and theologian.

know what to do if we lose focus along the way? In short, have we collected ourselves appropriately for the journey?

Before Jesus begins his public ministry, he ventures into the desert (Luke 4:1–13). It is an inward journey in which he encounters life's demons. In this story, he is challenged with the temptations of life, which include power, wealth, fame, and allegiance. Because Jesus is able to deal with them successfully, he frees himself from the ongoing distractions that can easily intrude on one's spiritual journey. This experience involves the preparation he needs in order to make his way to his spiritual base camp.

In many cultures, there are rites of passage from childhood to adulthood in which the individuals involved are asked to reflect on life questions. This period of exploration is designed to take the person back to spiritual basics and deal with the primary matters of life and belief. Such experiences are about centering.

Centering is the crucial beginning step in the journey toward spiritual wholeness. It serves as the compass, the ballast, the focal point that anchors life and provides a safe place to return to in times of difficulty and struggle. It also represents our base camp as we begin the journey. Without a strong sense of centering, one can easily become lost in the materiality of one's surroundings by either becoming overly distracted or by being obsessively preoccupied with physical things or surprised by unexpected challenges. The outcome of becoming distracted or preoccupied is to lose one's inner equilibrium, which is the place where centering should lead us. The problem today is that too many people aren't present where they are.

Centering is akin to the "Child's Pose" in yoga. It is the place or position to return to when needing to calm one's mind and body. In daily life, we need to find ways to center our spirit so we can deal with the ongoing activity and fullness of a dynamic world.

Over the years, when I've asked people, "When do you feel closest to God?" the answer more often than not is: "When I'm out in nature." I think this is because it is there, within the beauty of creation, that we are stopped in our tracks, overcome by the enormity of what we are a part of, stunned by a reality that we can't fully comprehend. Nature often forces us to stop, absorb things, and reboot rather than simply continue on our way. It may not be that this is where God spends the most time, but it is where we feel a part of something bigger than ourselves and our words simply aren't adequate to describe our feelings.

Centering has many dimensions to it. It begins with having a sense of openness and a desire to see the world clearly. When this happens, awe and wonder naturally follow. Centering is also about inner peace, being able to both give and receive, and understanding that both blessing and brokenness are natural parts of life, which need to be a part of our consciousness. This is how centering can lead us to a sense of inner equilibrium.

There are a number of important elements that help to make centering possible. We'll explore several of them here.

Openness

Openness has to do with accessibility and a lack of restriction. It involves receptivity, tolerance, frankness, and the avoidance of secrecy. Openness, in many respects, reflects a sense of curiosity.

Years ago, when I served as a church pastor in a small, rural community in Idaho, I remember one day traveling from Filer, where I lived, through a neighboring community, across a bridge that spanned the Snake River Canyon to another small town named Jerome. I was going there in order to attend a meeting that in actuality was almost directly across the canyon from my church. It was about a thirty-minute drive, because one had to reach a bridge first before crossing the canyon.

When I came back from the gathering in this neighboring town, I remember going to another meeting in my church that same afternoon. When I arrived, I told the group where I'd been and said, "I suppose you all have been to Jerome many times before, as well?"

One woman in the group turned to me and said, "Why would we go to Jerome, when everything we need is right here in Filer?" She was not joking.

It was an eye-opening comment and definitely caught my attention. It struck me as lacking curiosity and of being a bit closedminded. What do you mean, "Everything we need is right here in Filer?" I thought to myself. There's a whole world out there, waiting to be explored. Jerome is different than Filer, but you have to go there in order to figure that out.

One needs to have an open mind that you might learn something new, someplace else—something that you can't see or know from where you are. The truth is that this can happen to any of us regardless of where we live. The center of our world can revolve around New York or San Francisco just as easily as Filer, Idaho. What can I learn from those other folks? After all, everything I need is right here, in my community and world.

Kurt Vonnegut put it this way: "I want to stand as close to the edge as I can without going over. Out on the edge you see all the kinds of things you can't see from the center."[2] In order to be centered spiritually, you have to be willing to go to the edge of things, to see what you can't see from where you are standing currently. To be open and curious is deciding to venture to the edge to see what is waiting for you there.

In his wonderful book, *The Art of Travel*, Alain De Botton, calls this having a "traveling mind-set" and reflects on it in this manner:

> What, then, is a traveling mind-set? Receptivity might be said to be its chief characteristic. Receptive, we approach new places with humility. We carry with us no rigid ideas about what is or is not interesting . . . Home, by contrast, finds us more settled in our expectations. We feel assured that we have discovered everything interesting about our neighborhood, primarily by virtue of our having lived there a long time . . . We have become habituated and therefore blind to it.[3]

Openness is a key component in our journey toward spiritual wholeness, but it doesn't end there. If we are truly open, how do we receive the world that we explore?

Awe

In order to discover fully the qualities that are crucial to our spiritual journey, we need to turn from openness to the ancient concept of awe. Awe is "a feeling of great respect usually mixed with fear or surprise,"[4] and awe is at the very foundation of seeing the world spiritually.

Awe connects us to mystery. Awe reminds us that we are a part of something spectacular, which is ultimately beyond words. Awe blends the fear of the unknown with the overwhelming feeling of wonder that results from taking in all that we see and experience.

Without a clear sense of awe, it is easy for our lives to become too small and eventually be misguided by that smallness. This happens whenever we stop looking around at our extraordinary world and become satisfied with just focusing on ourselves, shrinking our view and making

---

2. Vonnegut, *Piano Player*, 86.
3. de Botton, *Art of Travel*, 242–43.
4. *Cambridge Dictionary*, s.v. "awe."

ourselves the center of our own spiritual, moral universe. When this occurs, we forget to acknowledge that we are part of something much bigger and grander than ourselves.

At the same time, without developing a sense of awe in our individual lives, our political and social structures become deformed. We lose our sense of humility and respect that naturally comes about when we encounter the beauty and vastness of the universe in which we all live.

In his book *Reverence*, Paul Woodruff says, "Reverence lies behind civility and all of the graces that make life in society bearable and pleasant."[5] Developing one's feeling of awe is what grounds our sense of reverence toward that which lies beyond ourselves. Awe, reverence, and wonder, taken together, ground spiritual life.

In a marketplace culture such as our own, in which everything is given a functional, utilitarian, or monetary value rather than a sense of sacred worth, the experience of awe serves as an important and transformative spiritual corrective to draw us back into a world that is larger, deeper, richer, and fuller. The spiritual concepts of awe, reverence, and wonder describe an essential truth that is common in nearly all spiritual traditions: life consists of a great mystery beyond our comprehension.

In the Hebrew scriptures, the writers expressed the belief that one cannot truly encounter God face-to-face because the experience is too overwhelming and awesome. In the few occasions when the divine-human encounter takes place, it is an intimate experience, as is the case between Moses and *Yahweh*. These stories describe what is taking place in this way:

> "But," he said, "you cannot see my face, for no one may see me and live." Then the Lord said, "There is a place near me where you may stand on a rock. When my glory passes by, I will put you in a cleft in the rock and cover you with my hand until I have passed by. Then I will remove my hand and you will see my back, but my face must not be seen. (Exod 33:20–23)

The sense of awe and reverence communicated in the special relationship that Moses had with his God *Yahweh* demonstrates that awe and ultimately humility are our natural human responses whenever we realize we are standing on holy ground, surrounded by the sacredness and mystery of life.

Awe isn't so much marked by a feeling of respect mixed with fear and wonder, as it is simply being aware that we are a part of something so beyond ourselves . . . so stunning . . . that there aren't words to describe it all.

5. Woodruff, *Reverence*, 5.

26

Feeling a sense of awe reminds us we don't need to define and classify everything in the world. Some things can be left unsaid, be allowed to reflect the mystery that is a part of life itself.

Sometimes we can become overly preoccupied with our own sense of power and think that we can create awe through material means or that it is the result of our own use of power.

A classic example of how those in power misuse the meaning of awe for political purposes was on full display in the form of American foreign policy in the 1990s and early 2000s, when we went so far as to title our war campaign in Iraq "shock and awe." The use of the term "awe" for military purposes was developed at the National Defense University of the United States to describe "the synchronous application of the full range of our national capabilities in timely and direct effects-based operations. . . against an adversary's critical functions to create maximum shock and disruption, defeating his ability and will to fight."[6] When the concept of awe is misused for political, economic, and military purposes, its spiritual power and moral value is lost to self-centered, human purposes. This misuse takes place in a variety of forms on many fronts today. It can be seen in everything from physical intimidation and abuse to hostile corporate takeovers. When we hijack the true meaning of awe for lesser, parochial purposes, we all suffer because we lose the collective value that occurs when there is a common understanding of the sacred nature of life that comes about when we truly encounter mystery and beauty. Awe is about things that are grand, which we have the privilege to experience on a regular basis.

In his classic work, *I Asked for Wonder*, Abraham Joshua Heschel summed awe up in this way:

> Awe is a sense for the transcendence, for the reference everywhere to mystery beyond all things. It enables us to perceive in the world intimations of the divine . . . to sense the ultimate in the common and the simple; to feel in the rush of the passing the stillness of the eternal. What we cannot comprehend by analysis, we become aware of in awe.[7]

When I served as a District Superintendent in the United Methodist Church from 2010 to 2015, I frequently drove through the beautiful Columbia River Gorge in Oregon and passed by the magnificent Multnomah

---

6. Blakesley, "Shock and Awe," 42.

7. Heschel, *I Asked for Wonder*, 3.

Falls along the way. Sometimes I'd stop just to take in its beauty as I headed on my way to various meetings.

As a result of this amazing experience, I wrote a poem to describe my own sense of awe at observing the power and grandeur of nature's beauty expressed by those falls:

Watching Creation's Sacred Dance at Multnomah Falls

Each droplet descends from on high,
cascading free-fall over the basalt ledge,
traveling hundreds of feet,
before plunging into the waters waiting below.

These wondrous acts
bold, majestic leaps
liquid, fluid, natural,
as if each drop is somehow aware of its part in the enormity of it all.

They take their turns
one-by-one,
joining together in the great mystery of life,
while embodying nature's heartbeat,
as they pulsate through the surrounding landscape.

And to think it all starts miles upstream,
as traveling companions
simple hydrogen and oxygen in liquid form,
gathering enough force,
making their way collectively through ravines and gorges,
as streams and falls,
responding to a primal urge,
to reach the ocean's aquatic burial grounds
before returning to their celestial womb
to begin nature's life cycle once again.

Timeless travelers
whose sweet song
transcends the human languages spoken below.

We simply look up in awe
speechless,
witnesses to this sacred dance
that moves from one to many
and back again.

Blessing and Brokenness

The spiritual journey is not just about what we receive. It also has to do with what we do once we receive and whether or not we notice everything that is around us. If we are fully attentive, we will become aware of both the blessings and the broken places that are a part of life. These components, taken together, help our centering experience to become real and balanced.

In spiritual terms, blessings have to do with those things that bring about well-being and a sense of joy in our lives. The natural response to this phenomenon is to feel thankfulness and gratitude.

Counting one's blessings is more than a math exercise; it is a spiritual discipline.

When I was a pastor, I often invited people who came to see me with discouraged spirits to start a blessing or gratitude journal. I gave them this simple instruction: Look for blessings in your life each day. Then make it a practice to write down one blessing you saw or experienced. Just one!

The individuals who did this simple exercise told me that when they first started, it was so difficult to see any blessings in their lives at all. Later, it became difficult because it was a problem limiting their entries to just one blessing each day! When we fail to notice our blessings, it is easy to ignore the fact that we have much to be thankful for.

Since January 1995, I have kept a blessing journal on a weekly basis. I now have a trunk full of these journals. What they depict is a very important part of my spiritual practice: Each Monday, I write down my blessings from the prior week and limit it to two short journal pages each week. Then every morning for the rest of that week, I read my blessings as a part of my morning routine.

The weeks are all different. Sometimes the blessings involve encounters with others. Sometimes they are as simple as recalling a walk in the neighborhood. Sometimes my blessings have something to do with what I saw or an aspect of life that was there all along but had previously been ignored. Sometimes the blessing represents a new epiphany or insight.

Part II: Four Qualities of Spiritual Wholeness

Why is this practice so important? Quite simply, because it has changed my life! I look for and notice different things about life than I did before. Since 1995, it has become a habit. At some point, counting my blessings moved from being *something I did* to becoming *who I am*—a person who sees blessings all around me.

It is important to note here that each of us will have a different experience with such an exercise. Our sense of blessing, as well as our experience with brokenness, is influenced on one level by our class, race, culture, life stage and experience, and a host of other factors. The material stuff involved is not distributed among us in the same way, but the spiritual qualities that are available to us are often quite similar.

I am a white middle-class male who is a part of the dominant culture in the United States. How I view and experience blessings and brokenness is impacted by that reality both materially and spiritually. Others, because of their own personal realties, will experience these important dimensions of life differently, which will impact how their spiritual narrative will be written.

I am not a refugee seeking political asylum and safety in a hostile world. I am not a person of color facing discrimination and racism on a regular basis. I am not a woman who has experienced sexual assault, harassment, or abuse. I am not someone living on the streets homeless. At the same time, I am not a person of great wealth or power. I do not hold a political position nor have celebrity fame. My experience of blessings and brokenness will be different from that of others.

This is true for all of us. Sometimes there will be seasons of great blessings and valleys of significant sorrows that affect how we might feel about this simple exercise of maintaining a blessing journal. Blessings aren't about comparisons with others. They have to do with one's ability to notice them wherever they are.

The reality is that there are countless people who possess great wealth and privilege who don't see the blessings they have in their lives materially or spiritually. There are those who live on the margins, who while struggling to make ends meet on a day-to-day basis find the riches of life in the midst of material poverty. Blessings and gratitude come in many different shapes and sizes, some are material, but most are spiritual in nature.

There are those with great power and wealth who act as if they are victims when things don't go their way. Then there are people, like George Dawson, who as a 103-year-old slave's grandson learned to read at the age of ninety-eight and wrote a memoir of his life experiences, entitled *Life Is So Good*. In the book, Dawson writes:

> Be happy for what you have. Help somebody else instead of worrying. It will make a person feel better. It's good to be generous. It doesn't take much to make a difference. Even the poorest man can just take time to say hello; that can be a help. Have some sympathy for someone's hard-luck story. It's not about money. Give what you can. And if you have nothing, at least pray for somebody. Have good thoughts.[8]

Dawson experienced a great many difficulties and challenges in life, but his perspective changed lives—his and those around him.

Counting blessings is not an easy thing to do. Life is filled with highs and lows. It is hard to pause, reflect, and value the blessings that are in one's life. But if we fail to develop this awareness and spiritual practice, it is difficult to ground one's spirit and reach out to others in meaningful ways. The awareness of our blessings, even in the midst of pain and struggle, is a crucial element to personal centering. It is one way spiritually to be a part of something bigger than ourselves.

At the same time, identifying places of brokenness in the world is a crucial companion to the spiritual practice of counting blessings. It serves to balance out our view of life. Without the presence of this spiritual counterweight, it is difficult to understand life or the situation of others fully. Life is made up of a variety of experiences, both enjoyable and challenging. Some people carry unspeakable brokenness that cannot be ignored. Having an awareness of both blessing and brokenness not only helps us reach a point of inner centering and equilibrium, but also engenders us with a sense of empathy and compassion for ourselves and others. At some point, we all encounter brokenness and we all experience blessedness. Both impact our spirits. Both center our lives.

Without being cognizant of our blessings, we miss the richness and beauty of life. Without being aware of the brokenness of the world, we lack understanding, compassion, and empathy toward the struggles and challenges that surround us. Blessing and brokenness, as spiritual insights, are connected in this way. One without the other leaves us incomplete and empty of the raw material needed to be fully grounded spiritually.

8. Dawson and Glaubman, *Life Is So Good*, 259.

Equilibrium

"Equilibrium is what makes life possible."

—JOHN POLANYI[9]

Centering should ultimately lead to a place of inner peace and personal equilibrium. Equilibrium has to do with our overall spiritual presence and how we ultimately settle the internal conversation that takes place between the competing interests and perspectives seeking our attention. If the spiritual toxins of closedmindedness, fear, revenge, selfishness, etc., gain the upper hand within our inner lives, then we lose our sense of spiritual balance. When we lack this kind of equilibrium, we easily become distracted or even dysfunctional and this inner state is reflected in our personal and social lives.

Because centering involves developing the capacity to see and experience life in non-material ways, equilibrium happens when we mature in this manner. In his classic book, *The Little Prince*, Antoine de Saint-Exupery says, "It is only with the heart that one can see rightly; what is essential is invisible to the eye."[10] Seeing rightly leads us to take a different course of action that is not seen with the naked eye. It has to do with what happens within the human heart.

While I was attending the Parliament of the World's Religion gathering in Toronto, Canada, in 2018, I heard a Buddhist monk speak about how his heart helped him see something that was invisible to the human eye. He spoke about the time he visited the border between North and South Korea and looked across the river to the north. While there was no physical wall between the two countries, it is clear that there was a very real border dividing them. But he felt a deep sense of compassion for the plight of the children living in the north and his heart was moved by the suffering taking place there. He told us that he wanted to do something about it. So, he said to himself, "If a border prevents me from seeing and helping starving children, what good is the boundary?" Once his heart spoke to him in this way, he decided to create a program, sponsored by his monastery, to assist starving children in North Korea. It was because this monk saw something different with his heart, which others simply could not see, that he was able to take humanitarian action.

9. This is a popular quote widely attributed to John Polanyi, a Hungarian-Canadian Chemist who won the 1986 Nobel Prize for Chemistry for his research in Chemical Kinetics.

10. de Saint-Exupery, *Little Prince*, 63.

This monk's experience poses an interesting question that results from the heart's seeing: What does it take—a border, a legislative action, popular opinion—to stop our hearts from seeing others as human beings who are deserving of our compassion and response? This question doesn't surface if we only see with our eyes. We must learn to see with our hearts as well. Seeing in this way broadens our view and expands our understanding.

Spiritual centering makes this possible, because by using our sense of openness, awe, blessing, and brokenness, our spiritual journey takes us to a place within where our inner equilibrium activates our heart, mind, and spirit to function in an entirely different manner. A centered, healthy spirit brings to our awareness the qualities that make it possible to see what cannot be seen with the naked eye alone.

The Buddhists and many of the indigenous cultures and traditions of the world understand the importance of equilibrium much more fully than we do as Westerners. Centering, balance, and stillness play a vital role in these traditions. In some traditions, equilibrium is said to be achieved through the practice of mindfulness.

Pema Chodron, the American Buddhist teacher and writer, puts it this way, "Mindfulness trains us to be awake and alive, fully curious, about *now* . . . The more you can be completely *now*, the more you realize that you're always standing in the middle of a sacred circle."[11] This sacred circle represents a state of equilibrium and peace anchored in the present moment. This is important within Buddhist thinking because it is how you become fully present to yourself and those around you. Thich Nhat Hanh, a Vietnamese Buddhist Zen master, says: "The practice of mindfulness is very simple. You stop, you breathe, and you still your mind. You come home to yourself so that you can enjoy the here and now in every moment."[12]

In the West we generally see this in much more functional terms. In the early twentieth-century, the American psychologist and philosopher William James was a part of the formation of a school of thinking referred to as American pragmatism, which focused on understanding the practical application of equilibrium in human community. Pragmatism concentrates on practicality and the application of how best to apply theoretical ideas to real-life situations. This approach to life involves a thoughtful, reflective stance toward the world that is grounded in rational responses, but also results in a sort of rational centeredness.

11. Chodron, *Comfortable with Uncertainty*, 116.

12. Nhat Hanh, *Silence*, 16.

James and others from the pragmatic school believed that critical analysis and thoughtful reflection led to moral responses that were the best ones suited for any given, specific situation. They were the most pragmatic choices.

Whether one sees equilibrium in terms of mindfulness or pragmatism, having a sense of centeredness is the core from which our responses are best grounded spiritually. Without inner balance, it is difficult spiritually to be fully present in the world. This is why the inward-out movement begins from a place of centeredness, which calms the inner spirit and leads to compassionate social action. This is how centering works from openness to equilibrium.

It is crucial that the various competing inner voices that seek our attention find a place of harmony so that our "better angels" can be expressed. This is what it means to live a life of spiritual equilibrium. When there is equilibrium in our lives, we are more likely to feel centered and whole.

For Further Study and Reflection

- Think about your childhood for a moment. What was an early interest you had that you have let go of? Is there a way you could open yourself back up to that interest and explore it once again? What would be the benefit in doing that?

- When was the last time you experienced a sense of awe? Where were you? Can you express that experience in words?

- Identify one blessing you've experienced today. Write it down at the end of the day. Do this exercise for a week. How did this experience change how you see things?

- What is one current social issue that "breaks your heart"? Is there something you could do to help alleviate this broken part of our society? Volunteer? Donate resources? Learn more about it?

- What would you need to do in order to bring about a better work-life balance and find greater equilibrium in your life? Is there one of these things that you could work with and begin to practice in the next month?

4
_____

Framing

Making Sense of the World

One thing I believe profoundly: We make our own history. The course of history is directed by the choices we make and our choices grow out of the ideas, the beliefs, the values, and the dreams of the people. It is not so much the powerful leaders that determine our destiny as the much more powerful influence of the combined voice of the people themselves.

—ELEANOR ROOSEVELT[1]

IF CENTERING IS ABOUT preparing ourselves for a spiritual journey, then framing involves wrapping our hearts and minds around a particular approach to life—creating a map of sorts—and then heading off on a path or way forward that leads us to our ultimate destination. Framing is something that we start to do early in life and then refine our framework again and again over a lifetime. In many ways it represents our inner default language because it involves our assumptions, basic values, and inner beliefs. It is more than just having a perspective on things, because when we frame reality, we have determined who our gods are and how we will relate to our world and others. Framing determines how and what we value and measure, whether it be material or spiritual.

1. Roosevelt, *Tomorrow Is Now*, 1.

35

If we return to the image of a mountain climbing journey, the concept of framing helps us consider a number of important questions: What can we learn from others who have made the journey previously? What are the various routes that we can take and which one will we choose to start our journey? What do we know about the experiences and history of those who have undertaken this trek before? How will we use our actual experience on the trip to adjust our assumptions along the way? How we view these matters and what framework we finally establish will significantly influence what happens next and whether we successfully complete the ascent. Framing matters, and each of us frames the world in our own way from an early age.

Centering Myth

When I was a local church pastor, I taught confirmation classes to young people, ages 12–14, as they prepared to become members of the church. In the first class session, I always told the group that if they only remembered one thing from our time together, they should remember this: *Everyone, whether they are religious or not, has a God in their lives . . . something that is at the center of who they are. What is at the center determines what they value, how they see and understand the world, and what they do with their lives.*

I know that this was a lot for a young person to take in, but the reality is that if, from the very beginning of our spiritual formation process, we don't understand the importance of framing and centering myth, then we will never understand the real meaning of life. In the process, we will allow others to determine our centering myth and life framework. Those who have political and economic interests are always more than happy to do this on our behalf because they get something of value from us as a result—either our money or our allegiance, or both.

Thomas Merton put it this way: "If you want to have a spiritual life you must unify your life. A life is either all spiritual or not spiritual at all. No (one) can serve two masters. Your life is shaped by the end you live for. You are made in the image of what you desire."[2] Like Merton, Jesus saw the issue of framing as paramount and addressed it again and again in his teachings. Jesus understood that people were either preoccupied with the material world or that they could learn to see things from a spiritual perspective, which was the focus of his Way. Jesus and Merton are not alone among

2. Merton, *Thoughts in Solitude*, 49.

36

the great spiritual wisdom teachers in addressing this basic polarity in life between the material and the spiritual and teaching about how important it is to unify one's inner life.

In 1858, Abraham Lincoln famously said "a house divided against itself cannot stand." He was referencing a statement that Jesus makes in the Gospel according to Mark 3:25. Lincoln, of course, was referencing the fact that the United States, which continued to struggle with the issue of slavery and union, couldn't be half slave and half free at the same time and remain intact. The frame of a building built on this basis would simply collapse under the incongruity of such opposite notions of freedom.

A few short years after his speech, the United States was involved in a great Civil War primarily because the American Founders, from the beginning, were unable to resolve the half-free, half-slave question. They were able to advance social thinking related to what a nation can be collectively in so many ways and called their accomplishment federalism, but because their framework included a fatal flaw, it ultimately led to civil war. We still deal with the consequences of this earlier flaw in our nation's framing through our ongoing racism and the creation of socially unjust systems that are racially biased.

The truth is what happens on a grand, social scale also happens on a personal level. We begin framing reality at a very early age. As time passes, that framing becomes who we are.

This reality reminds me of something that happened years ago, when our oldest daughter, Lindsey, was very young. One day, a neighbor friend of hers came over to our house to play. Annie was five years old at the time, and she enjoyed coming over.

On one occasion, my wife, Susan, was at her sewing machine, making clothes for Lindsey. While Annie was there, she became very interested in Susan's work as seams turned into sleeves and a piece of cloth began to look like something nice to wear.

After watching intently for some time, Annie turned to Susan and asked, "Why do you make things when you can go to the store and buy them instead?"

It was a reasonable question to ask. After all, stores do sell clothes, and you don't have to work in order to wear them. You just go and buy them at a store when you want something new.

However, Annie's question also demonstrates just how young we are when we begin to mediate life through a particular worldview. In this case, through consumer eyes that reflect an economic and functional reality rather than one that is personal and relational.

Annie could have asked a host of other questions from different framing perspectives instead. She could have asked: "Do you enjoy sewing?" "Who are you making that for?" "Can you show me how to sew?" She also could have commented on the quality of the work itself: "That's beautiful," or "I wish I could do that," or "Red is my favorite color." But instead, Annie's question took the conversation from our home to the nearest mall, "Why do you make things when you can go to the store and buy them instead?"

We develop the basic elements of our foundational framing and centering myths from an early age, and these assumptions get reinforced or challenged over time. As they do, they shape who we become, as we construct our understandings of life. We then interpret and shape our experiences through the assumptions and values we've formulated. Once we construct our worldview, that framework shapes us for years to come.

Framing involves the theoretical concepts that influence how individuals and societies organize and communicate reality for themselves. The frames that are chosen become our mental and spiritual representations of the world. Quite literally, these constructs become the places where we live.

These dynamics are central to understanding the spiritual nature of life. Every one of us has an interpretive lens that we use and that lens is ultimately a reflection of our God. Paul Tillich referred to this as our "ultimate concern." I see this more and more in terms of the foundational framing we use, which is based on our centering myth. This myth is the primary set of stories we create and the way in which we express that which we give value to and hold most dear. Our foundational framing is how we see things as a result of that centering myth. Muriel Ruykeyser put it this way, "The universe if made of stories—not atoms."[3] What is invisible to the eye has an impact on the world we construct for ourselves.

Both our centering myth and the framework that we create for our understanding of the world are shaped by our view of the world and what we see. This means that culture, class, racial, and gender-identity, and the role we play in society all have an impact on our eventual framework. Are we open to other cultures? Do we value the variety of expressions of gender? Do we value both feminine and masculine aspects of life? Do we notice and value people who occupy different stations in life? How we answer these questions will influence the framework that we create for ourselves.

3. Brussat and Brussat, *Spiritual Literacy,* 271.

Ultimately, these things are reflected in the words we choose and in our language. It determines how we define our world, and it begins with the words we use.

When Words Pour Out Like Wine

> When words pour out like well-aged wine,
> they tease the palate
> tempt the mind.
> Aromas and accents that fill our senses,
> transform our spirits,
> dissolve defenses.
>
> When words transport us
> on simple pallets,
> they carry us off to worlds unknown.
> Thoughts and ideas stacked one-by-one,
> form newfound meanings,
> help us be what we can become.
>
> When words explore the color of life,
> like so much paint on an artist's palette,
> they mix and blend
> one hue to another,
> transcending to what is yet unseen,
> connecting us to each other.
>
> Words . . .
> when strung together
> stretch our understanding,
> forming links between us, becoming art.
> Transforming, transporting, transcending the world,
> making their home in the human heart.

This is ultimately a theological task, but it is also something that each person needs to explore in order to understand the wholeness of what it means to be alive, spiritually as well as physically. This is what our ancestors did for millennia.

Theologians, scientists, and others talk about this in terms of cosmology, the ultimate framing, which deals with the nature of the universe. Thinkers from Plato and Kant to Albert Einstein and Stephen Hawking have influenced our discussion about the nature of the world. These discussions frame our cultures and influence how we use words and language to describe things.

Today, while we continue to focus on what divides us, we frequently fail to form any sense of a unifying, mediating narrative that can address the dynamics we experience in our postmodern world from a spiritual perspective. We do so at our own peril.

The biggest challenge we face to living a grounded spiritual life comes from the current context we live in. It is a setting that frames reality through the lens of the global marketplace that is primarily defined in economic terms. In a marketplace culture, everything material sheds its spiritual worth and gains value and meaning only according to its utilitarian worth. This becomes true for people as well as things.

Simultaneously, spirituality in this materially based world is removed from everyday life and is viewed as something peripheral to what is important, namely the marketplace. Central to this framing is consumerism, which makes its way into what we value and how we use our precious time: "Why do you make things when you can go to the store and buy them instead?"

The marketplace, consumer-framing lens depends on our desires for money, sex, and power to sustain it as the mediating reality within our world. These forces are all seductive, and when they become dominant in our lives, they turn us away from the fundamental spiritual principles that give life ultimate meaning.

Our spiritual task, individually and collectively, is to refocus and ground ourselves in a spiritually based centering myth that helps frame and mediate our world in a more wholistic way that is mindful of both the physical (material) and invisible (spiritual) dimensions of the world. Joseph Campbell put it well in *The Power of Myth* when he said,

> Mythology is not a lie, mythology is poetry, it is metaphorical. Metaphor, and the words and language that are used to interpret it, is found in mythic stories, and it is these stories that frame, and ultimately shape, our world. Once a centering myth is in place, it frames everything else.[4]

---

4. Campbell and Moyers, *Power of Myth*, 206.

Or as Howard Thurman says, "The place where you live is where your heart is. Where your treasures are is where your heart is. Where your heart is, is where your God is."[5]

But framing also takes place within a community context. Each of us ventures forth to understand and interpret the world in our own, unique way. The journey to acquire what one might call a worldview is deeply influenced by the community and culture we are a part of. The assumptions and language we use to frame things in the United States are not the same as they are for individuals living in China, Brazil, Kenya, or hundreds of other places. And even in our own country, our framework is influenced by where we live, our race and culture, our economic status, our education, work, etc. Each of us sees the world based on choices and decisions we make about what to value and what to ignore, but the ingredients involved in this discernment process come from the settings in which we live.

Vision Quest and Pilgrimage

In many of the indigenous cultures of the world, young people participated in vision quests in order to have the time needed to explore and experience life and ultimately to understand and frame one's life and come to terms with a sense of calling within it. In modern culture, we have forgotten about the importance of this sort of inner spiritual journey and its impact on framing and getting us in touch with the mystery of life.

Steven Charleston, who is a citizen of the Choctaw Nation of Oklahoma and ordained in the Episcopalian church and a teacher at the Saint Paul School of Theology, describes this experience in the following manner:

> The quest is the process, defined by every culture, by which human beings search for the holy . . . The Native American quest was pragmatic, designed to produce transformation. It was not a private esoteric experience, but a way in which the community prepared, supported, and developed functioning members of society. The quest was a tool, a method for seeding back into the community persons who understood both the spiritual nature of life and their role in it . . . The purpose of the quest itself is not to solve the mystery, but to deepen it.[6]

5. Thurman, *Deep is the Hunger*, 156.
6. Charleston, *Four Vision Quests of Jesus*, 10, 13, 15.

When I was a young boy, I didn't take a formal vision quest as such, but I learned at an early age that there were ways to enter into a different state of consciousness and connect with the holy.

This happened for me in different ways from reading inspirational works to powerful personal experiences. But it always meant putting myself in proximity to things that could help me enliven my spirit in transformative ways.

One of those ways had to do with music, when I made a startling discovery: I could transport myself into another state of consciousness by simply listening to powerful, soulful music for an extended period of time. Somehow, when this happened, I felt different and interacted with my world and others in fresh, new ways.

For me it was the music of Harry Belafonte and Nat King Cole that helped make this happen. It was as if their music "filled me with the spirit," so to speak, and I was transformed and changed. These were remarkable experiences that I relished, have never forgotten, and still practice from time to time.

I am not so naïve as to believe that I had gone on any kind of vision quest during these experiences, but as time has passed and scientific research has evolved, I am convinced that I was onto something back then that is significant and useful to the spiritual pilgrim.

Recent brain research is increasingly telling us just how remarkable and complex our brains really are. Things such as the practice of Buddhist meditation and listening to music can change our brain waves, that prayer alters people's feelings of health and well-being, and that viewing compassion or violence alters our brain chemistry in significant ways. These experiences are also a part of the spiritual quest that influences our framing of the world and our sense of centering myth.

Many religious traditions have long practiced the technique of spiritual retreats as a way to do this, and in recent times, there has been renewed interest in the ancient religious practice of pilgrimage. People head to Spain, England, Peru, France, and other "thin places" to discover, renew, and refresh their inner spirit. The goal of many of these experiences is to stop the normal patterns in life long enough to insert a different way of being. In the end, the hope is that this interruption will change one's view of the world, as well as the habits of daily living. The Spanish poet Antonio Machado put it best when he said, "There is no road, the road is made by walking."[7]

7. Machado, *Fields of Castile*, 149.

The spiritual journey is ultimately about one's ongoing search and renewal. It involves risk and challenge as we discover new insights that will transform our lives and help us frame reality in ways that anchor our spirits in deep, abiding ways.

Practice and Purity

Framing reality and undertaking our own spiritual quests naturally lead us to consider issues related to practice and purity. Both are tools for framing our experience. If we frame our sense of reality early in life and never alter it, we become stagnant and fail to grow any further. If we think that one's spiritual quest is a one-time event and involves reaching a particular destination, we will forget that spirituality involves a life-long journey. However, if we are open to daily experience, as it comes our way moment to moment, we will constantly be working to understanding what the world has to offer and maintain a sense of expectancy. We will explore the dynamics involved in this approach more fully in chapter 5.

One approach leads to the search for purity, while the other is about daily practice and the continuous process of pilgrimage and seeking. Both purity and practice are associated with spiritual life, but these two concepts take us to very different places.

Purity and practice are different expressions of spiritual life. The former focuses on certainty and right belief. The latter is about striving to improve through practice and spiritual discipline.

Purity, when it turns its attention outward, focuses on what others need to do in order to conform to my own way of believing how things should be. Practice, on the other hand, concentrates on the practitioner involved mastering various tasks in order to contribute something of value within the larger context.

Practicing spirituality should ultimately lead one toward a greater sense of simplicity. The problem with purity is that it quickly becomes complex, as more rules and procedures have to be added in order for one to remain pure.

E. Stanley Jones put it well in his book, *The Way*, which was written as a mid-twentieth century Christian resource dedicated to doing daily devotions. In one of the devotionals, Jones says, "Life for the Pharisee was very complicated. For Jesus it was very simple. The Pharisees lived by innumerable taboos, regulations, and laws. Jesus reduced these hundreds of laws to two: love to God and love to humankind. That is genius."[8]

Purity, especially religious purity, often leads to purges of one kind or another. At best, this means that those with power exile whoever they see as being less worthy and valuable, terminating conversation and damaging relationships in the process while making "others" expendable to the dominate framework and culture. At worst, purity results in actions that create a two-tiered system within society—the pure and the impure. When power is attached to it, purity easily leads to oppression or even ethnic, racial, or cultural cleansing. The current public discussion taking place about the nature of "white privilege" could be included in this, as well.

Purity also results in another form of spiritual failing: hypocrisy. Since no one is perfect and we all have things to work on in our lives, when someone focuses all their attention on being pure, it is often difficult to admit one's own personal shortcomings or failings for fear of being less than pure. This disconnect results in harshness toward others, while being blind to one's own behavior. Perhaps this is why Jesus summed it up so clearly with these words to the crowd, when they prepared to stone the woman caught in adultery: "Let any one of you who is without sin be the first to throw a stone at her" (John 8:7).

Striving for purity inhibits our journey toward practice, because it often focuses on what others fail to do properly. This happens because purity is preoccupied with correctness and conformity. Practice, on the other hand, is about humility and striving toward growth and maturity. It is an important part of the spiritual journey. E. Stanley Jones said in his book *Growing Spiritually*, "Spiritual maturity is no longer a luxury for a few; it is a necessity for us all."[9]

Practicing spirituality isn't easy. It requires much more of us than the search for purity does. Practice relates to our actions and involves our total being, not just our beliefs. Spiritual practice raises fundamental questions for us to respond to:

- How am I practicing what I hold most dear?

- How do I attend to my inner life and use my public voice?

- How do I honor my commitments to others?

- How do I embody compassion, kindness, and gentleness in my life?

8. Jones, *Way*, 288.

9. Jones, *Growing Spiritually*, vi.

The broader question is: How am I doing with living out my values? Practice requires constant openness—often conveyed with a sense of humility and a desire to improve—that recognizes that one is always in a state of formation. This process is always in motion, leading toward improvement and the mastery of particular, practical skills.

In practice, one is a participant. In purity, one is a judge. Practice, as a part of one's framework, while having a basic design, is always open to remodeling and new questions. Purity believes that once the foundation has been established it need not be questioned. Joan Chittister looked at these matters in terms of how we relate to basic questions: "We don't deal with major questions once. We deal with them over and over again, each time—if we're lucky—understanding them differently, learning from them more, dealing with them better, until our vision of them clears and our hearts calm."[10]

When St. Benedict set up monastic communities centuries ago, he outlined a number of factors he called "tools of the spiritual craft" that he encouraged the monks to embody in practical ways. These tools included everything from "speak no foolish chatter" to "pray for your enemies."[11] For St. Benedict, the monastery was a workshop or gymnasium for practicing the Way of Jesus, not a place for the pure to reside in arrogance toward others.

For there to be a restoration of spirituality in life, we need to become familiar with the notion of spiritual practice and find ways to make it a conscious part of our lives. Without practice, we will not be able to find our way from brokenness toward wholeness. This cannot happen by simply becoming purer.

If we are successful at centering ourselves spiritually and develop a framework that gives us a greater awareness of life being alive and sacred, then the next logical step is to put our understandings into practice in some particular ways so that we can integrate spirituality into our lives on a regular basis. Developing distinct spiritual qualities reinforces the framework we have created and helps us deepen our inward journey. This is how we will find our way forward along a path that honors those values we hold most dear.

10. Chittister, *Called to Question*, 227.

11. Benedict, *Rule*, 4.53, 4.72.

For Further Study and Reflection

- Draw a circle on a piece of paper. Write down the things that are important to you and identify the ways in which you spend your time. If you were to say what the one, most important factor is that you would put at the center of your circle, what would it be? Do your other activities, relationships, and time commitments reflect what you value most in life?

- Look around your house. Pretend you are an anthropologist. Determine what the objects in this place say about what is valued most by the tribe that lives here. List ten objects that catch your attention and write one sentence about what each item reveals about the occupants.

- What is one new spiritual practice that you would like to experiment with for one month? Try it out and then evaluate to see if this is something you'd like to make a regular part of your life.

- If you could create a pilgrimage experience, vision quest, or do a personal retreat, where would you go and what would you do?

- Part of spiritual life has to do with asking good questions. Consider these questions. Take some time to write down your responses:

  - Why am I here?

  - What legacy do I want to leave behind? How do you want to be remembered?

  - How do I relate to and treat those around me? What does my behavior say about my sense of humanity?

  - How do I use my gifts and talents? Who benefits from them?

  - What do I most want to do with my time on earth?

  - What do your responses to these questions say about your inner equilibrium? What do they say about the basic framework of your life?

5

Practicing

Turning Spiritual Principles into Personal Habits

Do what you can, with what you have, where you are.

—THEODORE ROOSEVELT[1]

IF ONE IS TO successfully ascend a great mountain, training is an important and prior step. One can do this in many different ways: reading about the experiences of others, spending time hiking to increase one's conditioning, and working out in the gym by climbing a rock wall. Each exercise helps get you ready for the real thing. It will also give you a sense of what your capacities and capabilities are. At some point, the repetition of your training activities is so ingrained that it becomes a part of one's very being. What you do in preparation at some point becomes who you are when you are actually climbing.

In the discussion about purity and practice, we learned that both involve our attitudes in framing a worldview. Each has to do with one's orientation toward life. But practicing is also a spiritual discipline.

In this section, we will pay special attention to those spiritual principles that need to become the personal habits we utilize along the way. Think about this in terms of hand and foot holds on a rock wall. Not all of the places you grab onto will take you along a path that leads you to the top.

1. Mason, *Conquering an Enemy Called Average*, 29.

Yes, there are lots of holds one can grab onto and there is more than one way to ascend, but some of the choices ahead of us lead to dead ends. When this happens, we need to be self-reflective enough to find new strategies to take us where we ultimately want to go spiritually.

The art of practice deserves special attention because it is through practice that our best intentions—and the centering and framing that they represent—become real. Without practice and the accompanying personal and social habits that are a part of it, our intentions remain theory and our desires continue to be dreams. Again, practice doesn't make perfect. Practice makes real, allowing the inward-out movement to reach fruition.

You can keep repeating the same steps in unsuccessful approaches, but in the end, they don't take you anywhere. When this happens, you can easily become frustrated by the experience, addicted to an unproductive path, obsessed by its initial promise and appeal, but that won't change the fact that the more you practice a meaningless strategy, the more you consume your time in an unproductive venture. In fact, you may end up deciding to give up the journey entirely, which means you would never experience the view from the summit.

The value of spiritual practice is that it gives you the opportunity to understand the different options before you better, notice the holds that can assist you with the climb, and give you the resources that you will need as you continue. In spiritual climbing, there are certain principles that are essential to developing a healthy spiritual routine. They apply to both personal and social spirituality.

Practicing anything from a sport to a musical instrument, from a physical skill to a spiritual discipline improves in quality as a particular behavior is repeated. Neuroscientists are teaching us that repetitive behavior also helps wire our brains and neuropathways in ways that result in those attributes becoming more natural over time. Charles Duhigg puts it this way in his book, *The Power of Habit*:

> ... the brain spends a lot of effort at the beginning of a habit looking for something—a cue—that offers a hint as to which pattern to use ... Over time, this loop—cue, routine, reward; cue, routine, reward—becomes more and more automatic. The cue and reward become intertwined until a powerful sense of anticipation and craving emerges. Eventually, whether in a chilly MIT laboratory or your driveway, a habit is born.[2]

2. Duhigg, *Power of Habit*, 19.

The goal of practice is not simply to turn principles into habits, but also to reach a point of spiritual insight so that we can modulate our own spiritual energy within a given situation at an appropriate and helpful level. When we do this effectively, the world around us changes for the better.

In terms of spirituality, practice isn't about perfection as the old adage "practice makes perfect" would have us believe. Instead, practice is about working to become more whole as a human being and learn the craft of living.

Let me use a story to illustrate this. Years ago, I wanted to learn some of my Dad's wonderful carpentry skills. I approached him one day after college and asked if he could show me how to build a cabinet from scratch. My Dad listened and replied by saying, "Let's start with something smaller first, such as a foot stool, so you can learn techniques like how to do tough and groove, which you'll also need for building your cabinet."

I wasn't thrilled by his response, but said okay, because I really wanted to build a cabinet and needed his help, since I was new to woodworking. As it turned out, the foot stool was not as easy as I thought it would be, so my Dad's instinct was correct—start small.

Once we'd completed this project, my Dad agreed to move on to building the cabinet. I showed him the design of what I wanted to make, and we bought all the materials needed. When we got ready to connect the top of the cabinet to the front and back, I measured . . . measured again . . . and cut. The only problem was that I'd accidently cut the large, top piece on exactly the wrong side of my design. When I tried to fit things together, it didn't work, and I got mad and used a few choice words to express my frustration.

My Dad looked at me patiently and said, "Don't worry about it. We all make mistakes like that. Put the top piece back together, and we'll just cover it up with some molding. No one will know you made a mistake at all, and besides the molding might even make it look better!"

My Dad was a good mentor. He taught music for a living, so I'm sure he encountered frustrated students all the time. By his words, he had reassured me as a novice at carpentry and convinced me that the project would still turn out okay. It did, and no one (except me and my Dad) knew that I had made a mistake.

During these two woodworking projects I learned a great deal from my Dad about carpentry, about patience, about self-acceptance, about life. I shouldn't have been surprised. Years before, when I was in elementary school, my Dad and I played tennis together. I always wanted to play matches, but my Dad would always say, "Let's volley for a while first, so you can work on your form and the placement of the ball. It will help your game."

Good spiritual mentors understand such things. Practice isn't about perfection. It is about developing one's techniques and personal habits. That is how you stay in touch with the spiritual realm. You practice.

Because of this, spiritual discipline should help us focus our attention on practicing those qualities of life that lead us toward wholeness. Start with small things before moving on to big projects. Learn to improve your form and placement before worrying about winning matches. We are on a mountain climb, so paying attention to the placement of holds along the way will help us in our ascent.

Let's look at some of the important spiritual qualities (i.e., hand and foot holds) that we can all work with and practice on a daily basis.

Gratitude and Giving

A good place to begin spiritual practice is with understanding gratitude and giving. Much like blessing and brokenness, which we discussed in relationship to centering, gratitude and giving need to work in tandem in order for them to take hold in our lives. While having a sense of blessing has to do with how one sees the world, gratitude has to do with the attitude one maintains in response to what is received. It's like the old saying, "We make a living by what we get, but we make a life by what we give."

The truth is that there are times when it is difficult to feel a sense of gratitude when life seems to be working against you. Gratitude is not about ignoring the difficulties and struggles one faces. Gratitude is about developing the spiritual discipline to look more deeply into the goodness that is also present, even when we find ourselves going through dark times in life.

Like breathing, gratitude is not a one-way movement. It involves both the act of breathing in to appreciate what one receives, as well as breathing out to find ways to give and share. Gratitude and giving work together in concert to complete this spiritual practice.

It is by being thankful and showing appreciation for what we have that we are able to turn our lives outward in kindness toward others. Today, this spiritual movement is referred to as "paying it forward." These words reflect the simple concept of passing along a good deed to someone else whenever you are the recipient of kindness yourself. It is a way to continue a positive chain of events. Anyone can do this. It is not a matter of one's class, culture, religious tradition, or political persuasion.

A saying that is often incorrectly attributed to John Wesley, the founder of Methodism in eighteenth-century England, reflects this sentiment as well: "Do all the good you can, by all the means you can, in all the ways you can, in all the places you can, at all the times you can, as long as ever you can." This quotation reflects the essence of what it means to fully integrate a spirit of gratitude in one's life so that it seamlessly leads outward toward service to others.

The spirit of the Psalm 23 reflects this sense of gratitude as well, when the psalmist writes, " . . . my cup overflows. Surely your goodness and love will follow me all the days of my life, and I will dwell in the house of the Lord forever" (Ps 23:6). These words depict a deeply grounded sense of assurance and thankfulness for the blessings of life. It is a reason to feel gratitude, which is a hallmark of the Jewish faith.

In fact, in the Jewish Haggadah Passover Seder ritual, there is a series of movements in the liturgy in which a blessing from God is recalled that is a part of the history of the Hebrew people. When it is described in the liturgy, the liturgical response of the people is: "It is enough." But then another blessing is recalled . . . and another and another. Each time the response is, "It is enough."

It is a way for those gathered to celebrate the Passover meal to remember the many ways in which they, as a people, have been richly blessed. Blessed beyond comprehension. Yes, it is enough, but then God offers still more!

I have thought about the ancient concept of gratitude through a more contemporary lens. Most of us are profoundly aware of the ways in which people experience Post-Traumatic Stress Disorder (PTSD). This condition identifies the very real, long term effects that are involved when people go through difficult, traumatic experiences associated with war, abuse, or other deeply disturbing life experiences. PTSD is something that deserves our awareness, attention, and caring response.

Perhaps what is true of trauma and stress is also true regarding goodness and gratitude. In terms of spiritual development, maybe we need to consider and experience what I call PGSD in our lives as well—Post-Gratitude Stimulus Dynamics (PGSD).

This is my terminology for the fact that just as people, who are deeply harmed by violence, tragedy, and stress experience very real psychological and spiritual consequences, they can also experience the lasting impact of positive qualities, such as love, compassion, and kindness which produce genuine feelings of gratitude within us. Increasingly, those involved in brain research are teaching us that the brain reacts differently to various stimuli, whether it is positive or negative, and that the result is a chemical change that takes place within the brain itself. Psychologists through their work with cognitive behavioral therapy and other mental imaging approaches have taught us that how we see situations has a profound impact on how we behave within them.

There are positive, generative attitudes, such as gratitude, that can help us stimulate our awareness, responsiveness, and how we process what is going on within and around us. If we are open to it, experiencing PGSD can make one positive thing lead to another. When this happens, our natural desire is to "pay it forward" whenever we can. Gratitude and a reciprocal spirit of giving are contagious.

The spiritual practice of understanding gratitude and responding with a spirit of giving is a crucial element in the spiritual journey toward health and wholeness. It is an important hand hold involved in the climb to the summit.

Humility and Kindness

A popular quote attributed to August Wilson says: "Confront the dark parts of yourself, and work to banish them with illumination and forgiveness. Your willingness to wrestle with your demons will cause your angels to sing." Through these words, Wilson reminds us that we are flawed, but precious, human beings. We are capable of great evil that can cause harm to others. We also have better angels that can change the world in positive ways. Coming to terms with this reality should help remind us that we are a collection of characteristics—good and bad—and like those around us, we are a part of a reality much larger than ourselves.

Humility isn't something that one achieves. It is a spiritual way of seeing ourselves in relationship to the world that helps us navigate our way through life. A spirit of humility presumes less and questions more. It creates a stance of offering our lives to higher purposes rather than assuming that we've already reached our destination. More often than not, we notice humility in others first and then try to embody this quality in our own lives.

One of the struggles we have in American society is that humility is seen as weakness. It is associated with vulnerability, which is not a characteristic that we are encouraged to develop. No one tries to persuade us to be humble. Instead, we're encouraged to be assertive, competitive, competent, and successful. Humility is portrayed as interfering with these traits, and being humble has an especially negative connotation, as in "eating humble pie." No one wants to do that!

In American culture, humility is something to be avoided, but we ignore this spiritual quality to our own detriment. While we often associate humility with saints, it is not a quality that the marketplace culture admires. While the material world sees it as innocent and naïve, humility is an extremely powerful spiritual characteristic.

Recently, I enjoyed watching the many tributes and documentaries related to the amazing life of Mr. (Fred) Rogers. In them, we see a man, who possesses great humility going about his craft of teaching children. Through it, we are able to see what this human quality really looks like. It is a marvel to behold, and it speaks directly to the spirit that dwells within. Perhaps this is why children responded so positively to Mr. Rogers.

Ironically, humility often appears as a trait in the lives of people who have very little means economically or politically. Somehow when one is stripped of material possessions, it is easier to understand one's place in a vast world of which you are only one part. Perhaps humility is more about personal vulnerability than it is about feeling in control.

This may be the reason why one of Jesus' most profound questions is "What good is it for someone to gain the whole world, yet forfeit their soul" (Mark 8:3)? The answer lies in something that Jesus says in another Gospel: "No one can serve two masters" (Mark 6:24). Humility is not about material gain nor political power. It is about spiritual wealth and understanding that one's light shines from the ground up rather than from on high.

Recently, in response to the Trump Administration's harsh attitudes, policies, and procedures related to the immigrant community in the United States, a number of volunteers in my community were trained to accompany immigrants as they make their way through the burdensome and often harsh conditions associated with the US immigration system. To do so, those of us who were trained in the accompaniment process were taught not to see our role as saviors to individuals who are victims of the process, but instead to be witnesses and supportive companions, trying to bring a humble, human quality to these situations and be with people as they journey through a difficult process.

In order for those trained in this responsibility to be truly helpful, it is necessary to learn what is often referred to as "cultural humility." It is easy for those who are a part of the dominant culture to feel like we know more, are smarter, and can fix things for others. But what does it mean to approach those who are being assisted as equals who are whole persons in their own right? How do those who have privilege in a situation work with others who do not, without treating them as victims or take away their own sense of agency and voice? This is not an easy thing to do. It requires a spirit of humility.

Humility has to do with seeing one's self and others as part of the larger world, and then find one's own proper role within a given situation, so that one's gifts and abilities are helpful, supportive, and sensitive rather than being domineering, arrogant, or superior.

Perhaps these words point us in that direction:

> Who am I to teach the world
> about how things should be?
> If you simply pay attention,
> the lessons are there to see.

> Life's a treasure filled with wisdom,
> where humility and beauty abound,
> and when we meet each other,
> we find ourselves standing on common ground.

Kindness naturally emerges in one's life, if humility is a part of our inner, spiritual core. A nineteenth-century Quaker proverb, sometimes attributed to Stephen Grellet, put it this way: "I expect to pass through life but once. If therefore, there be any kindness I can show or any good thing I can do to any fellow being, let me do it now, and not defer or neglect it, as I shall not pass this way again."

The spiritual quality of kindness can take place anywhere, anytime. Sometimes it comes in unexpected ways, but its impact lasts a lifetime. It too is a spiritual practice.

In his autobiography, *With Head and Heart*, Howard Thurman tells his personal story of trying to attend high school in the racially segregated Florida. He hoped to attend a church-supported high school for black children in Jacksonville. His family had contacted relatives there who were willing to put him up if he could get there. When Thurman went to the train station to make his way there, the ticket agent refused to check his bag because he told Thurman that he needed to attach the check for his bag to the trunk handle, but his trunk was tied together with a rope and didn't have a handle. The trunk would have to be sent express, but he didn't have any money to complete this transaction. Suddenly, a stranger, a black man dressed in overalls and wearing a denim cap, appeared before him and asked him about his problem. Then Thurman says this:

> "If you're trying to get out of this damn town to get an education, the least I can do is to help you. Come with me," he said.
>
> He took me around to the agent and asked, "How much does it take to send this boy's trunk to Jacksonville?"
>
> Then he took out his rawhide money bag and counted the money out. When the agent handed him the receipt, he handed it to me. Then, without a word, he turned and disappeared down the railroad track. I never saw him again.[3]

This in itself is a wonderful story about human kindness. But there is more. The story gains added meaning when you realize that Howard Thurman ended up being one of the greatest preachers of the twentieth century, the first African-American Dean of a major university in America, and a key spiritual guide to Dr. Martin Luther King Jr. and many others within the Civil Rights Movement during the 50s and 60s.

The power of this man's kindness shines through when you turn to the dedication page of Howard Thurman's autobiography, which was published a couple years before his death in 1981. It reads: "To the stranger in the railroad station in Daytona Beach who restored my broken dream sixty-five years ago."[4]

Kindness matters. It is remembered—frequently for an entire lifetime.

As you have learned by now, I have lots of signs in my office. One of them simply reads: "Practice Kindness." It is good advice. It matters. Do it.

There was a time, not terribly long ago, when you would see signs on car bumpers and other places that read, "Practice random acts of kindness." These words eventually developed into an actual movement in which people are encouraged to share kindness in their communities. More recently, I saw a sign posted at a church that read: "Humankind . . . be both."

3. Thurman, *With Head and Heart*, 24–25.

4. Thurman, *With Head and Heart*, [iv].

Kindness, like humility, is an integral part of living a spiritually-grounded life and creating a humane society. Without humility and kindness, life is unnecessarily harsh and inhospitable. Both are hand and foot holds along the journey. Both require spiritual discipline to become active in our lives.

Sex and Spiritual Connection

What does sex have to do with spiritual practice?

From *Gentlemen Prefer Blondes* to *Basic Instinct*, the latest romance novel to *Fifty Shades of Grey*, to *Playboy* magazine, to internet pornography, we are inundated with sexual imagery. But where do we learn the truth that sexuality is more about intimacy and mutual communion than it is about consumerism and conquest?

If sex were only about physical reality and had nothing to do with the spiritual realm, then why do we celebrate coming together at weddings to make promises and covenants with one another with the hope of sharing our lives "till death do us part"? Why do we believe that finding a soul mate and life companion is important? Sex is about more than SEX. Because of its profoundly intimate nature, it is about the very heart of what it means to be a human being. Sexuality is about closeness and matters of the heart. It relates to our spiritual lives as well as to the physical world.

Sigmund Freud was absolutely correct when he said that sex plays a significant role in human psychology and behavior. Think about it for a moment. From Kennedy, Hefner, and Clinton to Weinstein, Cosby, and Trump, inappropriate sexual behavior has been a part of the life of men in power in our country for quite some time.

Of course, we could cast the net much farther if we included the church's struggles with inappropriate and abusive priests and pastors, teachers taking advantage of younger students, and even an entire industry that we call human trafficking, which is a profit-making business. The development of the recent #MeToo movement has made us all more aware of the consequences of living in an overly sexualized society with new insight, even as women and men continue to be harassed and abused.

Sex, or what masquerades in its place, still fills the news pages and tabloids, and sex continues to be used in advertising and television programming. Sex is everywhere in our society. The question regarding spiritual practice is this: From a spiritual perspective, how do we relate to sex in a healthy and whole manner?

Sex will never find its proper place within our lives until it moves from being seen as having only physical value, much like any other commodity or object, to having spiritual value and therefore is appreciated for the intimacy and sacred role it plays within our lives.

While not all sexuality is about lifelong commitment and the institution of marriage, Joseph Campbell, in his classic work, *The Power of Myth*, points out the clear difference between the physical and the spiritual nature of sex and love:

> Marriage is not a love affair. A love affair is a totally different thing. A marriage is a commitment to that which you are. That person is literally your other half. And you and the other are one. A love affair isn't that. That is a relationship for pleasure, and when it gets to be unpleasurable, it's off. But a marriage is a life commitment, and a life commitment means the prime concern of your life. If marriage is not the prime concern, you're not married.[5]

Sex doesn't involve love unless it is pleasurable and enjoyable for both partners as equals and brings joy rather than harm into the world and human relationships. Healthy sexuality, when a part of a larger commitment, does this. Anything less is merely transitory physical pleasure, divorced from the spiritual world. In this way, sex has to do with spiritual practice, not just physical desire.

Individuals from a young age naturally explore and struggle with the role of sex in their lives, which relates to the very core of our being. How do I feel about the opposite sex . . . the same sex? What is my gender identity? When is a sexual relationship appropriate . . . consensual . . . sacred? Is intimacy about pleasure or commitment or both? Who am I really and how does sexuality reveal my essence as a person? What is my sexual orientation?

These are the personal, spiritual questions that make their way into the physical world based on our answers. Our responses impact our sense of happiness and wholeness. Excessive self-centeredness must ultimately give way to moderation and a willingness to understand someone else's wants and needs as well. It is the difference between a contract and a covenant, a transaction and a relationship.

This is where the presence of spirit comes in. Spirit serves as a moderating quality in life. On the one hand, it frees us to see things in new ways, while also helping to ground ourselves in those things we hold most dear. Our sexuality is one of these precious qualities of life that needs to be

5. Campbell and Moyers, *Power of Myth*, 200–201

handled with great care and responsibility. It connects us to each other in powerful and long-lasting ways.

Love and Listening

From here, it is only normal that we would move from a discussion on sex and human connection on a physical level to consider the nature of love and listening. These two qualities, when practiced, can have a profound impact on our lives. Rudy Rasmus provides us with a helpful definition of the nature and power of love:

> Love is both a feeling (noun) and a doing (verb). If you feel love, then you must do the loving thing. When you do the loving thing, then you feel more love . . . For love to flourish in any group, there must be a genuine appreciation for other people and opportunities to explore new relationships . . . Love requires a generous heart that is free of fear and a willingness to let yourself be known, even as you become willing to know others, including their unpleasant traits.[6]

This is not a new notion. The ancient Greeks had a number of ways to refer to love within their language and culture. There was *philia*, which had to do with friendship and affection—a virtuous love that reached out to others. There was *storge*, which had to do with empathy, and often referred to the love between parents and children or the love of country. Then there was *eros*, which we often associate with love, because it has to do with passion, sexuality, and physical attraction. And finally, *agape*, which is often overlooked even though it is at the heart of where the spiritual and physical worlds connect. *Agape* has to do with goodwill toward others and charity; it is the kind of love that spouses who are deeply in love feel toward each other.

In the Christian tradition, love is at the heart of its spiritual practice. The Apostle Paul wrote about the meaning of love to the Corinthians around 50 AD. The power of his words still resonates across the centuries as demonstrated by the fact that they are still frequently used as a reading at weddings. That's quite an accomplishment for an individual who was frequently arrested for attempting to live out his understanding of love as a part of a social movement in his day.

What did Paul say about love and why it matters? Here are his words:

6. Rasmus, *Love. Period.*, 3, 39.

> Love is patient, love is kind. It does not envy, it does not boast, it is not proud. It does not dishonor others, it is not self-seeking, it is not easily angered, it keeps no record of wrongs. Love does not delight in evil but rejoices with the truth. It always protects, always trusts, always hopes, always perseveres.
>
> Love never fails. But where there are prophecies, they will cease; where there are tongues, they will be stilled; where there is knowledge, it will pass away. For we know in part and we prophesy part, but when completeness comes, what is in part disappears. When I was a child, I talked like a child, thought like a child, I reasoned like a child. When I became a man, I put the ways of childhood behind me. For now we see only a reflection as in a mirror; then we shall see face to face. Now I know in part; then I shall know fully, even as I have been fully known.
>
> And now these three remain: faith, hope, and love. But the greatest of these is love. (1 Cor 13:4–13)

Faith, hope, and love abide, these three, but why is love the greatest of them? Simply put, because love, by its very nature involves our relationships with others, it inherently stretches us beyond ourselves. At the same time, Christian teaching tells us to "love your neighbor as yourself" (Mark 12:31), as a part of the Great Commandment, which means that love is a dynamic spiritual force that encourages us to connect in a loving way to ourselves as well as to others.

Love inspires us to relate in ways that lead to affection and understanding. Because of this, Paul believes that its power never ends. It is why it encompasses sex, while also being something much bigger and more profound.

Love isn't something that we store up for ourselves and then dispense when we feel like we need to do so. Spiritual qualities don't work that way. They are either a part of our lives or are absent. It's not that we always practice them effectively, but when love and the accompanying character qualities are developed well, they become a part of our consciousness. The spiritual practice involved is to do acts of love on a regular basis, not just when one feels like it or from time to time. In this way, sex is an activity that results from love, not the other way around. Love is a spiritual quality. Sex is a physical activity.

This means that love requires what Paul describes as the necessary elements of patience, kindness, truth, etc., rather than envy, boastfulness, arrogance, or rudeness. When love embodies these traits, it has the capacity to help us bear all things, believe all things, hope for all things, and endure all things. This is why love is so powerful. Look for and grab onto these holds as you make your ascent up the mountain.

In love, we depend on others, as they depend on us. This is the foundation of living a spiritual life. It is also the basis of creating a spiritually grounded society.

Today, we understand that love is expressed in a variety of forms. In his book, *The 5 Love Languages*, Gary Campbell speaks about this in terms of quality time, physical touch, gift giving, acts of service, and words of affirmation. Each of these expressions has a spiritual quality connected to it. We could also use words such as presence, communion, offering, kindness, and truth-telling to embody their meaning.

It isn't so much that we should approach life with a "live and let live" attitude as it is about being able to love and let love. This is no easy task. It requires the most we have to offer to others from the depths of our being.

When I got married in my early twenties, I married a woman I had met while attending college. We connected on a number of levels, and eventually got married. At the time, we cared about each other, had similar goals and ideas about life, and got along well. I thought that this relationship would last the rest of our lives.

But after nearly four years of marriage, it became clear that my wife was struggling with her own sexual orientation in profound ways, as she discovered herself becoming attracted to other women. When I first learned of this, it took me into a dark night of the soul experience. I needed to figure out what her self-discovery meant for me and my own sense of a lifelong commitment to someone else.

Needless to say, it took some time to come to the point in which I could answer the question: Do I love this person enough to step aside so she can become who she truly is as a person without standing in her way because of my own preconceived notions or needs regarding marriage?

This was not an easy journey for her nor for me, but our ability to see our love commitment as including our ability to let each other go taught me volumes about what real love is. Love is not about fulfilling one's own needs alone. It is not about sex or physical desire alone. It is a covenant with another human being that values that person's destiny and welfare as much as your own.

This kind of love requires us to listen closely to what someone else is actually saying. The problem, however, with human communication is that often an individual is preparing their response to the other person before letting them finish what they are saying. This means that I may hear your words, but I am not really listening to what you are saying. It took time for me to truly listen to what my wife was saying all those years ago.

Listening is a crucial part of growing in love. Edgar Schein calls it "humble inquiry," which is "the fine art of drawing someone out, of asking questions to which you do not already know the answer, of building a relationship based on curiosity and interest in the other person."[7]

This can happen only when one truly values the other person involved and tries to understand their interests and needs. This is the foundation upon which love is built. This is also what makes love more than a complex, one-dimensional feeling.

Love and listening both require us to ground ourselves at the very heart of who we are as human beings. People may experience love in very different ways, but in the end, it is as Paul says when he reminds us that it is the most important thing in life and will abide in the end. It takes practice to make this so.

Modulation

Lord, make me an instrument of thy peace;
Where there is hatred, let me sow love;
Where there is injury, pardon;
Where there is doubt, faith;
Where there is despair, hope;
Where there is darkness, light;
And where there is sadness, joy.
O Divine Master,
Grant that I may not so much seek to be consoled as to console;
To be understood, as to understand;
To be loved, as to love;
For it is in giving that we receive,
It is in pardoning that we are pardoned,
And it is in dying that we are born to eternal life.

—THE PRAYER OF ST. FRANCIS[8]

These practices of the spiritual life are all important, because, when taken together, they lead to a place where we are able to exercise the appropriate

7. Schein, *Humble Inquiry*, 2.
8. Prayer of St. Francis, often attributed to St. Francis of Assisi (1182–1226).

amount of spiritual energy for a given situation. In short, they become a path to the spiritual summit, which of course is also never ending. When we utilize these various tools in conjunction with each other, we are able to practice what I call the art of modulation. This art is expressed when our inner spirit and the spiritual tools we have at our disposal are used appropriately in a given situation.

All around us, we see people's inability to modulate their spiritual energy. Crowds march in the streets with guns, some angrily yell at others while in traffic, when people protest against injustice some individuals loot or promote acts of violence, the President of the United States tweets out disparaging comments that offend our spiritual senses and damage our social fabric, and people appearing on newscasts and talk shows interrupt each other without having second thoughts about it and yell rather than conduct civil conversations. We are surrounded not only by incivility, but by the lack of healthy, spiritually-grounded modulation. The impact of these circumstances adds to the overall spiritual imbalance in the world.

Some might think of this as simply a matter of self-control, which is a part of spiritual practice. But modulation is about more than this. Modulation is not only about restraint, composure, and moderation, it is also about understanding how much and what kind of energy to put into a given situation, so that it advances in a constructive manner. It is not simply about keeping bad energy out of one's behavior. It is also about knowing how to enter a situation productively.

When Richard Rohr writes, "If we do not transform our pain, we will most assuredly transmit it,"[9] he is not only describing the inward-out movement of the spirit, but he is helping us understand what happens when we fail to utilize the spiritual practice of modulation. What we fail to transform appropriately within us as positive, spiritual energy ends up creating negative energy, which damages our collective consciousness. This is not just true of pain. It is also true for anger, hatred, and violence.

Think about it in terms of the lunch counter sit-ins and the use of non-violence during the Civil Rights Movement of the 50s and 60s. Those spiritually-trained individuals were exposed to the cruel hatred and violence of Southern whites who taunted them, poured various things on their heads, and burned them with cigarettes. In response, they refused to act in like fashion. Instead, they were trained to find their spiritual center and respond non-violently in love. It was a remarkable display of spiritual modulation that had powerful social consequences.

9. Rohr, "Transforming Pain," line 6.

One might say that these Civil Rights advocates did this at great cost to themselves, but their spiritual modulation transformed their own natural human instincts in such a way that hatred and violence wasn't transmitted further. It had stopped in them and with them.

I think about this whenever I read Bishop Dehqanti-Tafti of Iran's powerful prayer entitled, "A Father's Prayer upon the Murder of his Son." In it, he says that God's last word is not about revenge, but reconciliation. It is not about adding to the hatred of the world, but about finding the most appropriate way to modulate one's spiritual energy toward redemption and healing.

Here is what Bishop Dehqanti-Tafti says at the conclusion of his prayer, following the murder of his son during the Iranian Revolution in the 1970s:

> O God, we remember not only our son but also his murderers; not because they killed him in the prime of his youth and made our hearts bleed and our tears flow; not because with this savage act they have brought further disgrace on the name of our country among the civilized nations of the world; but because through their crime we now follow Your footsteps more closely in the way of sacrifice . . .O God, our son's blood has multiplied the fruit of the Spirit in the soil of our souls; so when his murderers stand before You on the day of judgment remember the fruit of the Spirit by which they have enriched our lives and forgive.[10]

I cry every time I read this prayer, because it reminds me that in the end one's personal spiritual modulation, grounded and fully active, is about the essence of love, even when we find ourselves in the depths of despair and want to respond to hate with hate and violence with further violence.

The great wisdom teachers of the world tell us that there is another way that involves the spiritual capacities of gratitude and giving, humility, kindness, and love all working in tandem to help us find the best modulated path forward that moves toward healing, health, and wholeness.

All of us have a tendency to enter situations with our own scripts, plans, and assumptions. When we encounter other human beings, we have the opportunity to change scripts, alter plans, and revise our assumptions with new experiences, insights, and stories that become a part of the mix. We can choose to approach these situations in a variety of ways that relate to the spiritual practice of modulation.

10. Edelman, *Guide My Feet*, 72.

Modulation involves assessing a situation and discerning how best to invest one's spiritual energy and voice. It isn't just about what's going on inside. It has to do with how much spiritual energy to invest in things going on around oneself. Do I need to speak out or be more silent? Do I need to frame a question in a particular way that moves the conversation more deeply? Should I share a story that takes the conversation in a new direction? Or should I simply try to lighten things up? These aren't just personal decisions. They have to do with the spiritual practice of modulation because the path chosen impacts what happens next.

We have the freedom to choose how we enter situations, and we can modulate how we participate. This in itself is a foundational spiritual practice. We need to learn how to determine the proper amount of inner energy to add to a situation for the benefit of the common good.

For Further Study and Reflection

- If you could thank one person you know for one thing they've done to make your life better and more meaningful, who would that person be? What would you say? Can you set up a time to tell them "thank you"?

- Name one spiritual quality from another culture or tradition that taught you something special about the meaning of life. How might you utilize that quality in your life in the future?

- When were you last surprised by someone's kindness? What did they do? How did you react? What difference did it mean to you?

- If you are involved in a love relationship, what is a special quality your partner possesses that consistently draws you closer together? Have you ever shared your appreciation for that quality with your loved one?

- Next time you are in a conversation, rather than responding to something someone says, try asking a follow-up question instead to see what more the person has to share on the subject.

- Diagram a recent encounter you had that did not go well. Look at points within it where you could have chosen a different, more modulated response that would have changed the nature of the interaction in a more positive direction. Could you have responded differently? If so, how?

6

Living with Others

Engaging Life with Wholeness

In many ways, the saying "know thyself" is not well said. It were more practical to say "know other people!"

—MENANDER[1]

HAVE YOU SEEN THE National Geographic documentary film *Free Solo* about Alex Honnold's remarkable 2017 free climb up the face of El Capitan in the Yosemite Valley? It was produced by filmmakers Jimmy Chin and Elizabeth Chai Vasarhelyi and is the gorgeous, scary, and compelling story about this unbelievable human achievement. Viewing it is not for the faint of heart!

In this movie, we witness the story of the first person to ever successfully climb the 3,200-foot face of El Capitan without a rope. What an amazing feat. But while Honnold's climb is done solo, he is clearly not alone on this venture. There is his girlfriend, family, filming crew, prior climbers, professional colleagues, and all of us, who are with him on this quest as well.

It took Honnold two years to prepare for it and approximately four hours to complete it, which means that you better believe he had gone through the necessary steps of centering, framing, and practicing long before getting to this point in his personal journey.

1. Menander was a Greek poet (343–292 BC). Quote appears in Spier, *People*, [ii].

Honnold's climb is a reminder that even when we are pursuing our deepest personal dreams and undertaking our most challenging adventures, there are others who are with us along the way. Is the venture worth the risk? How do our personal decisions impact others? Clearly, there will be both risks and consequences to our actions. I think about the words of Honnold's mother, Dierdre Wolownick, in this regard, when she says, "I think when he's free soloing he feels the most alive, the most everything. How could you even think about taking that away from somebody?" Who we are and what we do affects those around us. It is part of the alchemy of relationships. We are constantly in a dance with our neighbors.

Because of this, living with others is about reaching out and making connections. It involves engagement and experiencing life in all its diverse, beautiful wholeness. It has to do with seeing where walls exist around us and between us and then knowing what to do in order to scale them or tear them down. If we are to build a more harmonious society, we need to change what we spend our time constructing and replacing walls, which cause division and pain, with bridges, which promote interaction and connection.

How we relate to others matters. At times, we might feel like we are climbing solo, but the truth is we are always living with others and we are not functioning in the world alone. We are instead climbing together. Today, many of our divisions have to do with us being disappointed that others don't see and interpret the world the same way we do. When this happens, we can become frustrated, often wanting to challenge and correct them for their wrong opinions rather than engage in deeper conversation. This approach usually results in an invisible wall being created between us.

How can we interact differently so that we enter relationships with others in a spirit of curiosity, having a willingness to listen and a desire to understand? At the same time, how can we give voice to our own opinions and insights, knowledge and understanding, perspective and beliefs? Balancing the two is not an easy task, but it is essential to living with others.

Understanding how to be with those around us is a natural outflow of the inward-out movement because it is the place where we discover the fullness of our humanity, as individuals and as a society. Henri Nouwen put it this way: "It is my growing conviction that my life belongs to others just as much as it belongs to myself and that what is experienced as most unique often proves to be most solidly embedded in the common condition of being human."[2]

2. Nouwen, *Reaching Out*, 15.

In order for this to become true, we need to see the barriers that create distance between us. Where there are walls, we need to create thresholds of connection. I wrote the following poem as a way to call attention to both the sacredness of our memories as points of connection while at the same time being willing to look at current contexts around us. Both qualities have to do with looking at ourselves in the mirror.

Reflections on a Wall

I.
In Washington, DC, there stands a wall,
rising up from holy ground and reaching to the heavens.
Obsidian black, appearing as a relic from the past.
Frozen in time . . . yet transparent,
obstructing no one's view of horizon nor self,
a reflecting pool of gathered faces.

This wall refuses to divide a divided time,
inviting us into its solemn sanctuary for a closer look,
quieting the noise of distant voices and troubled ghosts,
letting our souls search and soar,
recalling sacred stories,
putting current conflicts into proper perspective,
while uniting us with faces from another time and place.

Moving along this monumental pathway,
traveling from the living to the dead and back again.
Is this our past or our future?
This living shrine stands at the threshold,
where policies and lives collide and explode,
where allies and enemies are killed and maimed forever,
us and them, me and you.

Names upon names etched in granite,
precious, cherished, loved,
some 58,000 in all . . . brothers, sons, fathers . . . sisters too.
They are but a fraction of the total cost,
as families still grieve in distant places hidden from view.

Marked by memory, transcending time.
This is holy ground, where we meet ourselves once again,
and a giant rock becomes a melancholy mirror.

II.
In Arizona, there runs a wall,
not smooth like polished granite.
Shaped by steel and sharpened razor wire,
it blocks the sun and stills the air,
casting its somber shadow along a treacherous trajectory.

This wall defines a border,
refusing to be a reflecting pool for the soul.
It is a barricade,
stopping the movement of freedom and refuge,
constructed to cage those on both sides.
It too was built first by words and policies,
fixed in time and bound by the barrenness of our collective
conscience.

It stretches between neighboring nations and distant worlds,
measured in attitudes, not miles,
by height, not depth of understanding.
Piercing the heart, it turns kindness into fear,
as our better angels fly away,
searching for a more welcoming place to roost.

This is not a site of remembrance nor connection.
It stands alone to trumpet its own self-importance to those who
will listen.
Only the gathering of forgotten ghosts, some 10,000 strong,
can testify to this wall's success.
Lying lifeless in the sands,
no names immortalized in these deserts.
No monuments dedicated to their hopes and dreams.
This wall commemorates our own brokenness and separation . . .
among us, between us, within us.

III.

Perhaps these walls will one day meet
to call us all back home,
connecting now with then,
melting the divisions and assumptions of our hearts,
stopping us in their shadows long enough to listen and reflect,
letting precious names and the ghosts of strangers
mingle and get acquainted,
reminding us of the sacred shape of a human face.

Living with others means connecting, and this includes developing a sense of curiosity that leads to compassion and honoring covenants that create community. It also means being open to diversity and understanding when to be neighborly, when to keep appropriate "social distance," and when not to cooperate with structures and systems that divide and cause injustice. Finally, we must understand the connection that exists between justice and joy. Let's explore how to live with others in ways that develop relationships grounded in mature spiritual movement.

Curiosity and Compassion

Curiosity encourages us to go out into the world with an open spirit in order to learn and grow, while compassion is about connecting that spirit to those around us with a sense of loving regard and care.

Earlier I indicated that openness is a key element in centering our spirits. Curiosity plays a similar role in relationship to living with others. Curiosity is an open hand, open heart approach to living life as opposed to being one marked by suspicion and a closed fist. Curiosity, like awe, is a foundational part of living a spiritual life and is essential to personal growth.

Without curiosity, we easily become absorbed in ourselves, which is the first step in wall-building. It has been said that you can't learn anything new while you are talking, only when you listen. Curiosity is about listening to everything going on about you. It is easy, however, to lose track of the importance of curiosity in our lives. Ian Leslie puts it this way:

> Curiosity is vulnerable to benign neglect. As we grow older, we tend to become less active explorers of our mental environment, relying on what we've learned so far to see us through the rest of the journey ... If you allow yourself to become incurious, your life will be drained of color, interest, and pleasure.[3]

3. Leslie, *Curious*, xix.

Because of this, it is vitally important to remain curious in order to maintain a sense of connection and compassion in the world. This means asking questions, looking for new experiences and ways to encounter the world. It means setting aside one's preconceptions about how things ought to be. I have a quote I carry with me that says, "If you're not lost, you're not much of an explorer." Exploring involves risk, but also having the capacity to not always be in control. Sometimes when this happens, mistakes are made and you may even get lost along the way. This is the kind of spirit I'm talking about, because it allows room for interaction and newness to make their way into the equation. It is an important part of living with others.

When one is functioning with a sense of curiosity, both compassion and community become increasingly possible. I often think about this in relationship to the so-called discovery of the so-called New World. One historical perceptive is that the Americas were discovered by Europeans, but of course, there were others who already lived here before that happened. But once Europeans did arrive on the shores of what for them was a "new world," what attitudes did they bring to the situation? Did they embrace a world that was completely new to them or try to fit what they discovered into their own, preconceived notions of the world? How would things have been different in the interaction between these different cultures if the Europeans, who sailed on what was for them previously uncharted waters, had been more curious about what they discovered? Would this encounter have been different from the conquest and profiteering that ultimately occurred?

Curiosity expands and enlivens our world. A lack of curiosity compels us to force what we encounter to fit into our own image of things. In his book, *Curious: The Desire to Know and Why Your Future Depends on It*, Ian Leslie goes on to say, "Curious people take risks, try things out, allow themselves to become productively distracted."[4] Curious people also encounter people different from themselves and make it possible for authentic compassion to take place among us. Because of this, these two spiritual qualities are linked with each other in important ways. It is as if they are two important hand and foot holds that help us make our way up the side of the relationship wall we are climbing.

It has been said that "compassion knows no boundaries," and this is true. This is why it has many similarities to curiosity. Both curiosity and compassion involve the capacity of breaking through the divisions and distances that exist in the world so that we can truly meet one another.

4. Leslie, *Curious*, 17.

Frank Rogers, who has written extensively on the subject of compassion, says,

> Compassion is the heartbeat of humanity . . . Compassion is not about willing away unpleasant emotions or feigning politeness to those we secretly despise. Compassion is genuine loving regard that flows freely from the heart.[5]

Compassion comes from the heart, but also nourishes the heart, because it is the lifeblood of a healthy community. It encourages empathy and is a characteristic that moves toward connection. This is how community is built. Its opposite is intending to do harm, which ultimately leads toward alienation and disunity. This is why being compassionate is actually a spiritual discipline. It is a choice and a practice.

Today, we are at a point in our society in which our very survival depends upon our ability to develop compassion for each other so that we can break through our artificial boundaries and divisions. Our current trend toward tribalism and nationalism not only undercuts the spirit of curiosity, but it also disables our ability to feel compassion toward one another.

In 2008, recognizing the need for us to become more compassionate on a global level, the scholar and writer Karen Armstrong created and launched what is called the "Charter for Compassion." Since it was created, tens of thousands of people across the globe have signed on and participated in this charter, which states the following: "Compassion is no longer an option—it is the key to our survival. If our religious and ethical traditions fail to address these challenges, they will fail the test of our time."[6]

In order to make living with others a key part of our spiritual life together, curiosity and compassion are qualities that we all need to attend to and develop in tandem with each other. They form the basis of our relationships with others.

Covenant and Community

Covenant and community are likewise linked with each other spiritually as we establish commitments and promises with others in order to promote community and anchor our collective spirits. Like curiosity and

---

5. Rogers, *Practicing Compassion*, 9, 18.

6. Armstrong, *Compassion*, 1.

compassion, they are two of the holds that we must utilize to help us reach the summit of spiritual life.

To move from curiosity and compassion to a real sense of community, individuals must develop formal and informal covenants among themselves. The word covenant is both a noun and a verb. The noun means to have an agreement that is formal, solemn, and binding. As a verb, it means to undertake a pledge, a promise, or a vow.

The word itself comes from the Latin word *convenire*, which means a coming together. It assumes that two or more parties come together and agree upon some promises with each other. The concept of covenant is ancient and appears frequently in the Bible, being mentioned 280 times in the Hebrew Scriptures and thirty-three times in the New Testament. It is an important part of the Judeo-Christian tradition.

The concept of covenant involves a series of connections that sometimes overlap and can even conflict within one's life as we move out into the world. Our covenants most often begin close to home and expand outward from there. In fact, when you wake up in the morning and look into the mirror, your first covenant is staring you in the face. It has to do with the promises and commitments that you make to yourself as a human being and with the god that is at the center of your life. Covenants have to do with the very core of one's being, so if you aren't able to look at yourself in the mirror with a sense of inner peace and love, it will be difficult to live in harmony with others, maintain your commitments, or love your neighbor as yourself.

From here, it gets more complicated and begs the questions: How are you doing with your covenants with others? In your love relationships? With neighbors? In your community commitments? These commitments reflect your part in the social compact that holds our entire society together.

At times, it can be a challenge to hold our various commitments together in harmony. Today, we think about this in terms of our struggle with "life-work balance." It would be much easier if we had only a single covenant in life and could just call it good, but that's not how things work in a relational world.

"Coming together" doesn't just happen with a single relationship or in isolation from other factors in life. The truth is that we live in a transactional world in which we exchange goods, services, and time with each other every day, and there are a lot of competing interests.

Covenants play an important part in all this because they are not just about transactions, but about commitments, personal investments, partnerships, and "coming together" with others. They determine how we develop trust and respect between ourselves and others, which involve a deeper level of spiritual understanding and connection than simple transactions. Covenants demand that we don't overestimate our own importance, but also give attention to the needs of others and the agreements that we have made with each other. This is why the curiosity-compassion dynamic is so important to forming covenants.

Covenants are not about control, but about relationship. The systems scientist, Erich Jantsch, says, "In life, the issue is not control, but dynamic connectedness."[7] This dynamic connectedness is what makes covenants so vital to the success of community. In short, if we are not "coming together" with others, it probably means that we are "coming apart." This naturally leads us to consider the subject of community.

Community doesn't take place because a few individuals decide to practice "acts of random kindness" toward each other from time-to-time. Community is intentional and occurs when people seek to know and care about one another. It happens when individuals not only form covenants among themselves, but when their collective interests gravitate to those around them in ways that create a sense of trust and connection.

In *Creating Community Anywhere*, Carolyn Shaffer and Kristin Anundsen say that

> community is a dynamic whole that emerges when a group of people participate in common practices; depend upon one another; make decisions together; identify themselves as part of something larger than the sum of their individual relationships; and commit themselves for the long term to their own, one another's and the group's well-being.[8]

Everyone wants to feel a sense of belonging, that is, to be in community with others, but as Diana Butler Bass points out, this requires spiritual work, even if it may not relate to religious institutions. In her words, "Community is about relationships and making connections. That's spiritual work. And it may or may not happen in a church."[9]

---

7. Jantsch, *Self-Organizing Universe*, 196.

8. Shaffer and Anundsen, *Creating Community Anywhere*, 10.

9. Bass, *Christianity after Religion*, 193.

This work will require changes in ourselves and in our institutions. Robert Putnam pointed out in his classic work *Bowling Alone*, we need "a renewed set of institutions and channels for a reinvigorated civic life that will fit the way we have come to live."[10] While human beings depend on each other in essential ways, including the need for community, times are changing and how we connect with each other is not the same today as it was just a few years ago.

Technology and our sense of time and meaning have made us look at our relationships and how they are formed and maintained in new and different ways. The recent coronavirus pandemic and the future threat of pandemics will also change and challenge how we relate to one another. What will "social distancing" mean in a renewed, connectional world? Will my behavior in relationship to public health issues reflect a concern for my neighbor or only my own self-interest?

Interestingly, even in the work of community organizing, more and more time is being dedicated to relationship-building through activities such as talking with others in one-to-one meetings. Neighborhood organizations are built on engaging personal relationships.

It is clear that we need to develop a spirit of curiosity in order to increase our ability to be compassionate, and when we are compassionate, our covenants with one another become more deeply rooted. The natural result of this flow of spiritual energy is the formation of community among us. How this takes shape in the future is up to us.

These are the qualities that make for a wholesome society or as Parker Palmer put it: "A strong community helps people develop a sense of true self, for only in community can the self-exercise and fulfill its nature: giving and taking, listening and speaking, being and doing."[11] When we find our true selves and honor our inner commitments and social covenants, we are able to utilize our voices, while being open to the perspectives of others. If we continue on this journey together, the bonds between us will continue to grow. As we will learn shortly, these elements, taken together, serve as a fundamental part of the road toward justice, since they all involve creating enough space for all our voices to be expressed within the larger community.

10. Putnam, *Bowling Alone*, 401.

11. Palmer, *Hidden Wholeness*, 39.

Diversity

All men are caught in an inescapable network of mutuality, tied in a single garment of destiny. Whatever affects one directly affects all indirectly. I can never
be what I ought to be until you are what you ought to be, and you can never
be what you ought to be until I am what I ought to be. This is the interrelated
structure of reality.

—MARTIN LUTHER KING JR.[12]

Community cannot happen in a wholistic fashion unless we are open to
the diversity of those around us. Diversity involves including people from
different social and ethnic backgrounds, different classes, as well as different genders and sexual orientations. Today, we continue to understand
diversity in ever-expanding ways as we learn about each other more fully
through the power of communication and cross-cultural learning.

The spiritual task involved in understanding diversity and building
spiritual connection happens from person to person, and one encounter at
a time. Mohandas Gandhi put it this way: "I know that I cannot find (God)
apart from humanity . . . " He then goes on to say, "My firm belief is that
(God) reveals Himself daily to every human being, but we shut our ears to
the 'still small voice.'"[13] We are each touched by the brush of the divine, and
God is at work among us all. The task before us is to see the spark of the
divine in each other regardless of who we are.

When I was in the eighth grade, I remember reading George Orwell's
profound book, *Animal Farm*. It was a compelling read, and I will never
forget experiencing a feeling of betrayal in the story when, after rallying
all the animals on the farm against the humans and eventually gaining just
control under the banner of "all animals are equal," the pigs changed this
motto, once they gained power, to "All animals are equal, but some animals
are more equal than others."[14] This change reflects the temptation to under-
cut diversity with separatist, exclusive thinking.

One of the ongoing dangers in life, both politically and spiritually,
is to become closed-minded and feel more comfortable with the familiar and safe, rather than continuing to be open to the differences among
people or be willing to explore new horizons and encourage new voices to
be heard. There is a constant temptation to think that we are better than

12. King, *Strength to Love*, 70.

13. Kripalani, *All Men Are Brothers*, 57; 61.

14. Orwell, *Animal Farm*, 134.

others. In other words, while all of us are equal, some of us are "more equal" than the rest.

If diversity is an important spiritual value, then it is important to note that the opposite of diversity has to do keeping things fixed, uniform, the same. This can be true especially when power and privilege are at stake. It is easy to long for the safe and familiar in difficult and uncertain times, but the world is constantly changing from the molecular level to galactic dimensions. Our task, as beings within this changing world, is to learn about and explore the vastness of the world in which we live and be open to its diversity.

Our society grows and changes as we experience diverse realities and contexts. It has been said that "innovation happens at the intersection of difference," which means that if we are to progress as a society this can only happen when we encounter and ultimately embrace diversity and variety. When we fail to do this, we either simply stagnate in place or may even degenerate into a society that is unable to relate to its own unique contexts and challenges.

Because we frequently neglect to hear each other's stories, we don't realize that the cashier at the grocery store may be struggling financially on a month-to-month basis, or that the cook in the nearest fast food restaurant may be living in subsidized housing or need public assistance to make ends meet. We may not know that our family doctor has a loved one dealing with cancer or that a political leader is dealing with deep grief. Because we are so removed from each other, we no longer know who made our shoes or the conditions associated with garment workers or those working in meat packing plants.

The world is too complex to fully understand our surroundings, even though we need to know what is going on around us in order to create a caring, supportive community. In the absence of knowing and understanding, we default to what we think about others in terms of our economic relationships with them or our cultural understandings, which can distance us from our common humanity.

A wholistic sense of life that respects the diversity of our world is critical to our collective future. This requires us to truly understand what is taking place around us materially and spiritually, which means asking different questions than we usually raise about where we live.

How well do you know your neighborhood? Who lives there? What cultures are they a part of? Who is involved in caring for the children? Who employs your neighbors? Are those who work in your community treated fairly? Do you know those who aren't your own age?

Do you know anything about the watershed you are a part of? Where does the water come from? Is it clean and in good condition? How does your community's use impact those living downstream?

When we interact with different opinions, perspectives, and cultural traditions, we not only learn something new about others, but also have the opportunity to reexamine our own assumptions and beliefs, and we can adjust them, as needed, to face new realities.

Whenever we encounter something different, something new emerges. This dynamic is related to the German philosopher Hegel's concept of dialectical methodology, or what is referred to as the thesis, antithesis, synthesis formula, which means that something new and different arises whenever there is an encounter between two different perspectives.

Today, to our detriment, many see the growing interest in diversity and the creation of a more open society that honors cultural and gender differences as being about "political correctness." What this perspective means for those who use it is that we are unnecessarily being forced to pay attention to various perspectives in a "politically correct" manner in order to be polite.

Unfortunately, this falsely grounded, pejorative categorization of diversity and openness preserves the position of privilege for those who already have power and maintains a stance of closedmindedness toward those who are different from ourselves. Viewing diversity through this narrow lens diminishes conversation, encourages distancing judgment, and obstructs understanding between people. It is an effective, objectifying political tool that damages community and undercuts the collective sense of spirituality between people.

In the end, it is a deadly force, which is at work in our world today. Think how different things would be if we were able to say to each other, "Tell me more. Help me understand your experience, without telling me what you believe to be true." Community is built through the willingness to converse with each other in order to learn and understand.

Diversity is about developing one's inner capacity to encounter everything and everyone with a sense of openness to see others as special and sacred, even if they are not exactly like me. For us to move in this more wholistic, spiritual direction, we will need to develop a spirit of curiosity that removes narrow-mindedness and judgment and replaces those traits with genuine compassion, trust, understanding, and love.

If this spirit can be developed within our body politic itself, we will make major strides to eliminate bigotry, incivility, and violence. This is not an easy task. It will require genuine conversation and social action at all levels of government that removes the institutional walls that exclude and divide us from each other.

Neighborliness and Non-cooperation

If curiosity and compassion, covenant, community, and diversity are essential elements to develop one's spiritual principle of living with others, then it is important to understand that in the larger social picture these qualities relate to both neighborliness and non-cooperation. Let me explain.

A foundational quality of the spiritual life, as expressed in the Christian tradition, has to do with understanding Jesus' story of the Good Samaritan (Luke 10:25–37). This story challenges us to consider how we treat one another and raises the question: Who is my neighbor?

It also demonstrates that the answer to this question is defined in spiritual rather than geographic terms. In fact, Jesus' story breaks down traditional boundaries between people and exposes bigotry, condescension, and acting like a bystander as profound acts of unneighborly practice.

In his story, Jesus declares that you either move toward the person on the roadside and respond to the needs of a stranger, sharing what you have to offer . . . or you pass by on the other side of the road, neglecting your neighbor. There is no middle of the road when it comes to being a real neighbor to those around us. This is a case when, as they commercial says: "Just okay is not okay."

A bystander is someone who is present at an event without participating in it. It is easy to become a bystander in life even without intending to do so. All you have to do is watch things happen and not engage in what is going on around you. In matters of spirituality, such an approach to life is unacceptable since all of life has spiritual value and is connected. To understand who my neighbors are, and respond to their needs, means being fully present in the world.

However, in matters of ethical consciousness, when we come into conflict with the prevailing political policies and practices of a society that are unjust or that harm innocent people, to be a bystander is to participate in what is being done and treat it as if it were acceptable. History is filled with examples in which the conscience of people has led them to stand up and resist governmental or social norms that they see as harmful, unjust, or oppressive.

Several years ago, when my wife, Susan, and I were visiting Amsterdam, we stayed in the old Jewish Quarter and saw a number of important sites there that marked the Nazi occupation of the city in World War II. One of those sites was the Dutch Resistance Museum. In this powerful museum, visitors were constantly confronted with the question: What would you do if you were in that situation—adapt, cooperate, or resist?

This is not some theoretical question. It was and can still be very real and immediate. In those years, the answer that countless individuals decided upon had a dramatic impact. In 1940s Amsterdam, of the 107,000 Jews who lived in the city at that time, only 5,000 survived the Nazi concentration camps. Clearly, many people simply adapted or cooperated with the Nazi's policies in order for that to happen.

At the same time, of the 25,000 people who went into hiding (including Anne Frank and her family), 18,000 of them survived. This meant that many of those living in Amsterdam during those years made personal, risky, and significant choices to protect their Jewish neighbors or strangers.

These individuals answered Jesus' question "Who is your neighbor?" in a profound way that saw the common humanity of their neighbors who held different religious beliefs. Instead of cooperating with those in power, who had created policies and practices that where harmful and led to oppression and death, they resisted. These Amsterdam citizens decided not to cooperate with injustice, violence, and oppression, even if those in power said it was governmental policy and the way things should be.

Their decisions were spiritual in nature. But it is important to note that many religious people chose to go along with things and adapt rather than refuse to cooperate or resist injustice when they saw it.

We are a part of the society in which we live. As a result, our actions matter in relationship to the greater whole of which we are a part. Sometimes, in spite of our natural desire to connect and reach out to others, our spiritual principles call for a response of non-cooperation, even resistance.

Classic examples of this run the gamut from Thomas Beckett to Thomas More, from the American abolitionists of the nineteenth century to Martin Luther King Jr. and the Civil Rights Movement of the 1960s, from Gandhi's liberation movement in India to the various liberation movements of Latin America. People of conscience have taken the opportunity to stand up, sometimes against overwhelming power, in order to bring a sense of spirit and justice into the public arena. It is a part of spiritual living, and when it happens, spiritual energy breaks into political realities with great power and force.

I think about this today regarding our nation's policies toward immigrant families who are seeking asylum and freedom from violence and oppression in their own countries, only to reach the US border and have their children separated and taken away from them. What would you do if you witnessed such a thing—adapt, cooperate, or resist? Or what about the situation of police violence toward people of color—the African-American community, in particular?

Martin Luther King Jr., in his "Letter from a Birmingham Jail," put it this way:

> I am in Birmingham because injustice is here . . . (and) injustice anywhere is a threat to justice everywhere . . . I submit that an individual who breaks a law that conscience tells is unjust, and who willingly accepts the penalty of imprisonment in order to arouse the conscience of the community over its injustice, is in reality expressing the highest respect for the law.[15]

Countless individuals over the centuries have reached the same conclusion, and this spiritual insight forced them to see neighborliness in a fresh new way as they decided to take steps of non-cooperation and resistance in order to be true neighbors to others. Who is your neighbor? Are you willing to stand up when they are being mistreated or oppressed?

It is so easy simply to adapt to injustice or inappropriate behavior in small, subtle ways and then realize later that we contributed to the behavior by becoming a bystander, failing to speak up or take a stand.

In the 1990s, I served as the pastor at a church that had a men's group that met regularly. Often at the meetings, there would be a few members of that group who would tell jokes that were culturally insensitive.

One day, after one of their meetings, the only African-American member of the group came to my office. He looked deeply troubled and wanted to talk. I invited him in.

This is what he said: "I feel terrible about what happened at the meeting last night, and I wanted to apologize to you."

At first, I wasn't sure what he was talking about, but he went on: "At the meeting, I told a joke that made fun of Chinese people, and I am very sorry I did that. I feel terrible. Will you accept my apology?" He then said:

15. King, *Letter from Birmingham Jail*, 3.

"I've always noticed that when those kinds of jokes are told in the group that you never laugh and seem unhappy about it. I'm sorry I told that joke and feel badly if I offended you."

I told my friend that when inappropriate jokes were shared, I always felt uncomfortable and told him I appreciated his apology. I also said how grateful I was that he came in to see me and share his feelings. It was not lost on me that the only person of color in an all-male group would be the only one who recognized what was happening and was willing to come to me and say that he was uncomfortable with what was taking place.

What has troubled me over the years since that conversation is this: It's one thing not to laugh at something inappropriate, but it is something else altogether to find a way to change a culture that is responsible for inappropriate things being said in the first place and in the process letting them continue to be acceptable and normal. Was not laughing the best I could do in those situations? Did I somehow think that would make it stop? Or, was something more than that required of me? Couldn't I have stood up in some other way to express non-cooperation and resistance? Looking back on things, I felt like I should have apologized to my African-American friend for not doing more at the time.

To this day, I feel a sense of responsibility for not doing enough. I had adapted when I needed to resist. It is so easy to do. Things that are offensive can become normal and acceptable all too quickly. And soon those qualities become the foundation upon which further injustice toward others is built.

Joy and Justice

Joy does not simply happen to us. We have to choose joy
and keep choosing it every day.

—HENRI NOUWEN[16]

Let us realize that the arc of the moral universe is long,
but it bends toward justice.

—MARTIN LUTHER KING JR.[17]

16. Nouwen, *Here and Now*, 29.

17. Martin Luther King Jr. used this phrase often in his sermons. A similar expression was also used by Theodore Parker, a Unitarian minister and abolitionist, in a sermon entitled "Of Justice and the Conscience" in 1853.

In order for the spiritual principle of living with others to be fully realized, we need to come to terms with two concepts that all too frequently are not seen as being related to each other—joy and justice. What do joy and justice have to do with each other? And how are they related to living holistically with others?

I have to admit that I didn't fully grasp their relationship with each other until I invited a friend to lead a Bible study at the beginning of a conference I was hosting on "Poverty and the Church's Role in Justice Work." My friend didn't begin his teaching at the conference that morning with a familiar justice-oriented scripture verse such as Jesus' words, "Whatever you do to the least of these, you do unto me" (Matt 25:40). Instead he began by reading these words written by the Apostle Paul to the Philippians, "Rejoice in the Lord always. I will say it: Rejoice. Let your gentleness be evident to all. The Lord is near" (Phil 4:4–5).

My friend then went on to say that a joyful spirit was an important mark of early Christian witness in the world. He continued, saying that if today we can't do justice work and relate to those experiencing poverty with a joyful spirit, then we should not be doing that work because those living in poverty have enough struggles in their lives without having to deal with our joyless acts of service. Wow!

Serving the poor and doing justice isn't just about our material responses to others. It also has to do with the spirit in which that assistance takes place. If joy isn't a part of our spirit and action, perhaps it is received as a burden rather than as a gift! This simple teaching has to do with the human spirit both as individuals and in relationship to others.

If helping others is simply a matter of handing out food or building Habitat housing, and if there is no joy or human connection involved, then why are we doing these things in the first place? Joy cuts through the marketplace culture we live in and brings us toward one another. It adds a sense of dignity and community to our actions. It moves us from doing a transactional service to making a personal relationship. Despair, guilt, and hopelessness are not able to do the same thing. Both approaches are contagious and both have an impact on what happens among us.

I think about this in terms of something I learned years ago, when I was leading a Volunteers in Mission Team to work at a United Methodist site in Louisiana. Our group took a day off in the middle of our work week to visit the nearby Tabasco factory located at Avery Island. This is quite a place, because it produces nearly all the Tabasco sauce marketed in the United States.

As it turned out, just as our group arrived at the factory, a school bus pulled up filled with elementary-aged school children who were also about to tour the facility. Even though we wanted to get through the factory first and avoid all the commotion of doing a tour with young children, we ended up on the same tour together. This turned out to be a real blessing.

As it happened, when the tour was completed, the guide asked the entire group, "Does anyone have any questions?" Suddenly, a very enthusiastic young boy raised his hand. When the guide called on him to see what his question was, the boy shouted out, "This is the best day ever!"

Who knew? Could it really be the best day ever? And why not? His response put a smile on my face, and I have told this story countless times over the years, only to see my listeners smile as well. The young boy's joy on that day expressed great enthusiasm and energy, and his delight became contagious well beyond when it first occurred.

Doing justice in the world is hard work. It has to do with seeing the world in a wholistic way—as it really is. This does not always result in feelings of joy. Sometimes seeing the world as it is can be an eye opening, troubling, discouraging experience.

For example, when you think about the fruit and vegetables that you eat every day, how often do you think about the farm workers who picked them? When you think about the clothes that you are wearing, how often do the countries of Vietnam, China, Cambodia, Sri Lanka, or Bangladesh come to mind? When you think about who built your house, how often do names like Jorge, Francisco, or Manuel come to mind? When you use your computer, did you consider the fact that immigrants played a significant role in making this advanced technology possible? When you eat out at a restaurant, how often do you remember what country the service staff that works in the kitchen or that buses your table came from? Do we notice those who serve us? Are we aware of their life situations? Are we concerned about justice for them and their families?

Injustice happens because all too often we either don't notice or we accept the reality of today as if there is no better way and believe that we cannot shed the hate, violence, oppression, and abuse that makes things the way they are in our world. This happens whenever we convince ourselves that human trafficking and sweat shop conditions, economic inequity, and racial violence cannot be eliminated from our lives.

In her classic dystopian short story, "The Ones Who Walk Away from Omelas," Ursula Le Guin confronts us with the spiritual toll involved in accepting things as they are by describing a happy society that exists because they've made a devil's bargain that allows a single child to live in misery as if the child is an "it." As Le Guin says in her story,

> They all know it is there, all the people of Omelas. Some of them have come to see it, others are content merely to know it is there. They all know that it has to be there. Some of them understand why, and some do not, but they all understand that their happiness, the beauty of their city, the tenderness of their friendships, the health of their children, the wisdom of their scholars, the skill of their makers, even the abundance of their harvest and the kindly weathers of their skies, depend wholly on this child's abominable misery.[18]

It is hard to hear the truth and harshness of these words, even when they describe our current reality so clearly. We have come to accept the economic disparities among us as if it is okay for a few to build personal wealth and construct economic kingdoms for themselves while others work multiple jobs and still find themselves and their families unable to make ends meet or, even worse, end up homeless. Justice begins by first seeing those around us, acknowledging their presence, and making sure that they are treated fairly and with respect.

We have been conditioned to see success in our country in economic terms and seem confused when, centuries later, Jesus' words, "What good is it for someone to gain the whole world, yet forfeit their soul" (Mark 8:36)? still describe the world we've created. It is as if we'd rather build walls to keep this truth from us rather than work for social justice and fairness for those who have been marginalized.

Leo Tolstoy put it this way, "I sit on a man's back, choking him and making him carry me, and yet assure myself and others that I am very sorry for him and wish to ease his lot by any means possible, except getting off his back."[19] It is time to get off the backs of those who work hard and still can't make ends meet by creating a society that treats all people with dignity and respect no matter their cultural background or economic status.

You may be familiar with the story related to the African Zulu greeting *Sawubona*, which means "I see you." When you say this word to someone you meet, the response to the greeting is *Ngikhona*, which means "I am here" or sometimes translated "It is good to be seen."

---

18. Le Guin, *Unreal and the Real*, 5–6.

19. Tolstoy, *What Then Must We Do?*, 54.

This exchange implies a relationship of dignity and a willingness to notice each other's real presence in the world. To be noticed is to have significance in life. To be ignored is to be diminished spiritually. Greeting one another is the beginning of human connection, even between strangers and passersby.

Ironically, in the midst of the "social distancing" practices that have entered our consciousness in the aftermath of the coronavirus pandemic, I have found that people, while maintaining their distance, have increased their capacity to see and greet each other. It is a positive sign in these turbulent times.

Those who participate in yoga are familiar with this sign of acknowledgement and respect as well, when teacher and students use the expression *namaste*, which in Sanskrit means "the spirit in me honors the spirit in you," at the conclusion of their time together.

Beyond seeing, living with others means standing up for each other. The Hebrew prophets were known for their commitment to matters of justice as well, and their words speak across the centuries, oftentimes with force and generally directed to those in power, who have the capacity to change things at a structural level:

- "Woe to those who make unjust laws, to those who issue oppressive decrees, to deprive the poor of their rights and withhold justice from the oppressed of my people, making widows their prey, and robbing the fatherless. What will you do on the day of reckoning, when disaster comes from afar? To whom will you run for help? Where will you leave your riches" (Isa 10:1–3)?

- "This is what the Lord says: Do what is just and right. Rescue from the hand of the oppressor the one who has been robbed. Do not wrong or violence the foreigner, the fatherless or the widow, and do not shed innocent blood in this place" (Jer 22:3).

- "He has shown you, O Mortal, what is good. And what does the Lord require of you? To act justly, to love mercy, and to walk humbly with your God" (Mic 6:8).

These are more than passing words offered to a distant God. These are prophetic pronouncements spoken by a people longing to live in a just society.

Living with others is a complicated proposition. Diversity and covenants, power and justice, walls and bridges are all a part of the dynamics of how we come together or fall apart. Things in life don't always go well or as one would like. Our task as spiritual pilgrims is to learn how to move toward each other rather than moving away from those around us. The goal is to find ways to build relationship and community so we can live in harmony with our neighbors.

It begs the questions: Who are my neighbors? How can I build relationships with them in a spirit of joy? Our responses to these questions will determine the kind of people we ultimately become.

For Further Study and Reflection

- What is one thing—a travel destination or locale, a new experience or activity, a class or educational opportunity—that you've always wanted to experience but haven't? Are you curious enough to try this new adventure in the coming year?

- Who are the primary people you have covenant relationships with? What role do they play in your personal community? What could you do to strengthen these connections?

- How might you connect with someone outside your normal personal network? What questions would you ask that individual about their life and world?

- Is there a time you can remember when you were able to do justice work in a joyful manner? What difference do you think it made to *you*? What about to those you were working with?

- When was a time you stood up against an injustice you saw in the world? How did you feel? What did you do? What difference did it make? Would you do it again? Are there any situations of injustice that you see today that you would like to take action on? What could you do that would make a difference?

PART III

Navigating Times of Political Turmoil

IN ORDER TO SHIFT the focus of our lives and culture from political division and brokenness to spiritual understanding and wholeness, it is necessary to literally "work out" together and "work with" one another within the framework of the social realities that surround us. This redirection and cultural shift will not come easily, especially when new challenges such as "social" or "physical distancing" are involved. The political brokenness of our current state of affairs is so deep that we even argue over wearing masks as a public safety message, as if protecting one another has to do with political ideology rather than human responses to matters of public health. It will require something significant and deep within us to change our current state of affairs and move beyond our tendency to treat deep spiritual matters as if they are simply political in nature.

As we have already seen, there are lots of temptations, distractions, and disruptive forces at play. Many would rather the world function in a divided, disruptive, and inharmonious manner because spiritual disorder keeps the *status quo* in place and maintains a system that values the material and physical over the spiritual and ethical. Those who benefit from this way of living in the world will not give up their power nor the framework that supports it without a fight.

The principle of spiritual practice reminds me of why it is so important to develop a workout routine, exercise regularly, or go to the gym each week when a person decides to become more physically fit. One cannot reach their goals nor full potential without working out regularly and being a part of an environment that makes it easier to get into shape. Going to the gym frequently and building relationships with others who are there helps support our commitment to do this while expanding our connections with others who have a similar interest.

Prior to the coronavirus, when I went to my gym, I was surrounded by sayings on the walls that read: "Be strong," "Believe in yourself," "Every minute counts," and "Be beautiful in your own way." These statements, and countless others written on the walls of the workout rooms, create a supportive, empowering environment that reenforces the desire to become more physically fit.

The same thing can be said about one's inner well-being and the shift that is needed to move from the material to the spiritual. As the next chapters reveal, this will require us—individually and collectively—to confront a number of assumptions, barriers, and challenges that have driven wedges between the physical and the spiritual realms, as well as between each other.

We will begin by looking at several universal challenges, then focus our attention on some uniquely American problems that must be confronted and overcome for us to become more spiritually grounded. We will conclude with two chapters dealing with how to navigate these obstacles. One relates to addressing conflict in healthy ways. The other is about discovering one's life calling so that we can each be a part of a larger movement toward change.

We must learn to name and claim the issues we face in order to confront them effectively. We must also find helpful ways to move forward together. As Parker Palmer says, "Nations, like individuals, have myths rooted deep in their histories, myths that are always contradicted by their complex realities."[1] If we are to move from a marketplace culture to a world more embedded in spiritual principles, we will need to address the myths and social challenges that are currently blocking our path.

1. Palmer, *Healing the Heart of Democracy,* 178.

7
_____

Barriers to Making Progress
in Our Spiritual Journey

CENTERING, FRAMING, PRACTICING, AND living with others are not
spiritual disciplines that happen in isolation. Context matters, connecting matters, and conversation matters in order for these qualities to gain
meaning and become rooted in one's life.

Before turning our attention to the current social challenges within
the United States that make it so important for us to rediscover our sense of
spirituality in times of political peril, it is important first to address several
realities that we face more broadly as individuals. These realities are more
universal in nature and always play a role in how spirituality develops and
is lived out in different contexts. I will look at them through an American
lens, but these components have a more global quality to them that is expressed differently throughout the world.

Racism, Sexism, and Homophobia

Without question, the violence that racism does to the human spirit is debilitating and devastating, both to the one to whom it is directed as well as
to the individual displaying the racist behavior. Racism diminishes the soul
and smudges the sacred image of everyone involved.

It is a social disease and affliction that is expressed individual to individual, but becomes rampant when it is institutionalized. This has happened
in most every society in one form or another from European colonial rule

to South African Apartheid from the various Asian wars that have taken place among the Japanese, Chinese, and Koreans dating back centuries, to the forms of American racism, which include everything from taking away land and life from Native peoples and making them outsiders in their own country, to enslaving African people and forcing them to come to a distant land only to be enslaved.

Racism, like any disease, crosses political boundaries and infects everything and everyone in its wake. The trauma it causes is lasting and results from an abuse of power and the violation of the rights of others in ways that turn neighbors into strangers, turning them into something "other." It produces both political and spiritual consequences, and ramifications both social and personal. It involves everything from the use of words of diminishment and ridicule of a person's humanity to the involuntary servitude of others. It damages the wholeness that is so essential to the spiritual realm because it assumes that someone else is less than me simply because of their color or culture. This premise changes one's frame of reference in a fundamental way at its very foundation from one of openness, curiosity, and worthiness to one marked by closedmindedness, indifference, and disrespect. This shift in framing denies the spirit the air it needs to breath and function within us.

Racism always has consequences, often in terms of the loss of human life, as the recent deaths of Tryvon Martin, Eric Garner, Michael Brown, Tanisha Anderson, Ahmaud Arbery, Breonna Taylor, and George Floyd all attest. The list of names seems endless. Lives all lost at the hands of racist violence—often at the hands of police officers. And it is not isolated to a single community within our country. Racism, in America, touches down everywhere it can gain a foothold: Ferguson, New York, Milwaukee, Atlanta, Los Angeles, Minneapolis, Portland, Louisville, and Birmingham. The list of names and places seems never-ending and it is heartbreaking.

Racism is not new and has been embedded in our social systems from the very beginning, as the 1857 Dred Scott Supreme Court decision and our current Jim Crow system of mass incarceration make clear. Each version of racism legalizes discrimination against others while creating castes among us. What is institutionalized in our physical world through laws and systems is internalized within our hearts and spiritual lives as well. There is always the temptation to think that we have moved beyond racism, since in the United States we had a Civil Rights Movement or because we elected our first African-American President. But racist attitudes and behaviors seem to always linger within a society, and we need to constantly reexamine and challenge ourselves regarding our sense of being awakened. Our work is not so much about what we have done in the past as it is about what we will do next.

Like racism, sexism has similar, spiritually debilitating consequences. It diminishes others, while ignoring the fullness of life by overlooking the feminine components that make life healthy and whole. It often includes the abuse of power toward a particular group of individuals as earlier feminist movements, the #MeToo movement, and the LGBTQ movements can all attest.

Politically speaking, sexism and homophobia often result in things such as unequal pay, the lack of women in positions of political and economic power, and discrimination toward those who have different sexual orientations. In more recent years, as our awareness of the fluidity of sexuality, gender identity, and the rights of LGBTQ individuals have come into greater light, these factors have meant everything from fighting for the simple awareness that there is a range of sexual orientations and expressions within the world, to honoring the social rights of people to be who they were born to be.

Like racism, sexism and homophobia are often systematized and institutionalized so that the social responses of a society not only deny individuals their basic rights, but often lead to denying them their ability to personal expressions of life, liberty, and the pursuit of happiness that, as Americans, we believe are central to personal and social well-being. Sometimes this is true even to the point of experiencing violence and physical oppression.

Spiritually, these hostile expressions toward others result in the diminishment of the human spirit and deny society the wholeness that comes from having a more open spiritual understanding, since the fullness of life and the diversity of the world is not allowed the freedom needed to express itself completely. Patriarchy has often played a significant part in this dynamic within religious circles through the use of narrow, traditionally masculine language and by maintaining social control that narrows the imagery associated with the sacred while preserving a traditional, male-dominated governing structure. While there has been progress in this regard in some settings, we still have a long way to go for these dimensions to advance our social understandings and practices.

If the centering images and the use of language that are a part of our spiritual life do not express the full sense of our understanding of sexuality, it is a given that our spirituality will likewise be restricted and diminished. The tragedy of this is that not only will we continue to create social barriers among us, but we will lose out on the depth of human meaning that comes when the spirit is allowed freedom to help us understand each other.

As we have said throughout this book, the rediscovery of the spirit needs to have the qualities of openness, curiosity, and an ability to listen to and learn from others if we are to truly find an inward-out movement that is spiritually whole and has a social and political impact.

In his classic work, *A Different Mirror*, Ronald Takaki puts it this way: "America's dilemma has been our resistance to ourselves—our denial of our immensely varied selves. But we have nothing to fear but our fear of our own diversity."[1] A key factor in healing our souls and moving from political brokenness to spiritual wholeness will be addressing the chains of racism, sexism, and homophobia and overcome the damage that is done because of it.

Spiritual exploration:

- What are your earliest memories of relating to someone of a different race or culture? What were the challenges involved? What new understandings about life did you gain?

- When you consider the words that describe your images of spiritual life, what words come to mind? Do these words utilize masculine or feminine imagery? How do they reflect the values and characteristics that you hold most dear?

- When you consider the friendship circles of your life, who has been a part of them? What role have these individuals played in your sense of what is most valuable to human connection? How diverse have they been?

Class Matters

The second barrier relates to class. You need not be a Marxist to realize that people live in drastically different economic realities. Some people live in mansions and have multiple homes, while others live in trailer parks or even find themselves living in tents on the streets. In the United States, the

---

1. Takaki, *Different Mirror*, 427.

median national income is approximately $61,937 (2018).[2] This means that half of the people in the country live above this amount, while half live below it. When you consider the situation that many face in the economy, you clearly see a disparity between those doing well and those who are struggling. This reality also breaks down along racial and gender lines, which only reenforces the disparities and problems mentioned above.

The dramatic impact of the coronavirus on the economy has laid bare these many inequalities within the United States, but most other countries have their own version of this sad story. The destabilization that has resulted from COVID-19 will affect economic stability for many years to come. What it means is still difficult to fully comprehend, but without a doubt it will only add to the disparities that we see today, unless we choose a different path.

It is one thing to talk about rediscovering the spirit and live a balanced, whole life, but if people are not able to move beyond their own class reality and understanding, it will be hard to change our society as a whole or make spirituality a key part of our communal life. The challenges people face regarding spirituality are quite different if they are trying to make ends meet on a daily basis, as opposed to having too much wealth and struggling with what it means to have material excess and maintain one's connection to humanity. It is easy to overlook how economics and social isolation impact how we experience life and see each other.

A simple example of the reality of class barriers can be seen in two grocery stores located near my community. One is WinCo, which is an employee-owned store that has good prices, a diverse customer base, bulk bins, and a bag-your-own-groceries style that creates a levelling quality between cashier and consumer.

The other store is located nearby. A shopping mall stands between them. This second store is New Seasons, an upscale grocery chain that has lots of organic options, tends to be located in gentrified neighborhoods, and draws a wealthier customer base. Both are fine stores, but they are not the same. Those who shop in each come from different social circumstances.

The divisions between these stores are striking. They are of an economic, not political, nature. You can see the two stores standing near to each other from the road, but they are located worlds apart.

For the most part, the people who frequent these two stores are not the same economically, and when they finish their shopping, they go back

2. US Census Bureau, *American Community Survey, 2018.*

to their separate neighborhoods and often lead lives that seldom touch except in transactional, service-related ways.

Some of our class divisions are much more complex than this, and sometimes they are invisible to us.

I remember years ago, when I was just fourteen, taking a Saturday afternoon drive with my brother on a country road not more than fifteen minutes from our house. Along the way, we came across several migrant labor camps. I had never seen anything like them before and was shocked by what I experienced.

Here were several rows of simple, rundown shacks located next to open garbage pits. Local agricultural workers, who picked the berries and other produce in our area, lived in these places with their families. I couldn't believe what I saw and ended up doing a Junior High School project on my experience called "Invisible in Washington County." I simply didn't know that people were living in conditions like that, especially in a nearby community.

While some of these conditions have changed over the years, others have not. Many of the people who are located in such places still live in fear and often are neglected within our society, even as they harvest our food, prune our Christmas trees, and are involved in many of our construction trades.

On a global scale, all we have to do is look at the labels on our clothes to realize that in terms of many of our everyday basics and essentials, we simply don't see the entire picture. Garment workers from places around the world provide us with the clothes we wear. What are their working conditions like? Do they receive adequate pay? Are their rights respected?

And what of the meat packing plants, coal mines, shoe factories, and restaurants from coast to coast? Are those who make these industries go paid well, treated fairly, respected? These questions aren't new to American society, but because they seldom enter our public consciousness, they aren't given the attention they deserve from our spiritual understanding and reflection.

Class matters in our world, and it's a reality that separates us from each other in fundamental ways that impact our individual and collective spiritual well-being. In many ways, these realities represent one of the most basic ways we "otherize" and separate ourselves from one another.

If our personal, spiritual journeys are to go deep, we need to become more aware of what and who is around us, as well as understand that we will never see things fully. Sometimes we simply aren't able to understand life in its rich, complex variety, but if we practice the spiritual qualities we discussed earlier, we can begin to pay greater attention to the needs and realities of others.

Spiritual exploration:

- How could you learn more about and interact with people from a different class than your own?

Faux Freedom

Another barrier we face today is what I call *faux* freedom. There has been a lot of discussion in recent years about "fake news" and "fake facts," but we have a societal infatuation and problem with faux or fake freedom as well. This phenomenon is growing among us and is seldom discussed. It is especially strong in the United States, which prides itself on freedom, but it manifests itself in other societies as individuals seek out personal identity in social contexts.

Faux freedom results when we lose track of what freedom is truly about. Sometimes, those with a severe case of faux freedom even see themselves as victims, when in reality they are individuals with great agency and power. Unfortunately, President Trump represents this perspective on a regular basis, as he continually complains publicly about being treated unfairly, even though he is one of the most powerful leaders in the world. Faux freedom can happen anywhere, but generally has a self-centered foundation.

Freedom is about one's ability to make choices and live without undue or oppressive constraints. It involves intentionality, as well as desire. It reflects our ability to lead independent lives within a larger social context. It is an important American value and was so important to the American Founders that nearly all of them spoke about the importance of freedom regarding our young nation.

Viktor Frankl, who experienced the oppression of Nazi concentration camps during the Second World War, put it this way:

> We who lived in concentration camps can remember the men who walked through the huts comforting others, giving away their last piece of bread. They may have been few in number, but they offer sufficient proof that everything can be taken from a man but one

thing: the last of the human freedoms—to choose one's attitude in any given set of circumstances, to choose one's own way. And there were always choices to make.[3]

Freedom involves our ability to choose, but it can also involve great sacrifice and sometimes even the risks involved in an escape from oppression or abuse by others. Many of those living in war-torn countries today are exercising their freedom to emigrate in hopes of finding better circumstances for their families. Freedom is a deep human yearning.

Faux (fake) freedom confuses what real freedom is all about. Fake freedom has to do with making choices about less significant matters and can even involve a sense of experiencing imaginary threats to one's own freedom when that's not really at stake, which leads to feeling oppressed over matters that pale in comparison to those related to real freedom.

For example, I have the freedom to take a long, hot shower and may complain when the hot water runs out, while others don't have the freedom involved in having enough water to quench their thirst. It is easy to have lots of freedom about simple things and end up taking things for granted, while ignoring the realities of others who are facing real struggles related to their freedom. A marketplace culture amplifies this falsehood through the promotion of excessive consumerism for those who have the means to use their freedom as they wish, while others struggle with the basics.

Exercising one's freedom in a *faux* manner can also be aggressive, denying others their own sense of freedom and safety. This can occur through the carrying of weapons in public display as a way of intimidating others from exercising their own opportunities to voice their opinions. Others yell or flip you off while driving if you get in their way, feeling they have a right to the road and you are a barrier to their freedom. Some individuals send out aggressive emails or Twitter responses because "I just want to speak my mind." Personal freedom is not about exercising aggression toward others in ways that demand silence nor the denial of someone to be present in the world.

Such understandings of freedom are misguided and damage the spiritual sense of community. True freedom always has to do with how one's own rights interact in relationship to others in the community they are a part of. One's personal exercise of freedom can actually deny someone else their freedom, because freedom doesn't just move in one direction. It is interactive and either builds a free society or results in the oppression of others.

3. Frankl, *Man's Search for Meaning*, 104.

Oftentimes, "fake freedom" has to do with the false belief that I can simply do what I want in life and that no one else has the right to contradict or stop me from doing what I wish to do. This understanding of so-called freedom is growing among individuals living in our communities.

When real freedom turns into "fake freedom," oppression and brokenness are often the result. Unrestrained freedom for one person can lead to abuse, oppression, rape or violence toward another human being. In political terms, this is why the American Founders were so concerned about human ambition and put in place structural checks and balances within their governmental system to blunt the effects of "fake freedom."

As noted earlier, Howard Thurman said in his book *The Search for Common Ground*, "I have always wanted to be *me* without making it difficult for you to be *you*." Freedom is about deep, personal desires, but it is also something that we need to work on together as a community, understanding the fact that others may have different desires from me. Real desire isn't a small thing, but in a society of plenty, we can easily lose track of our desires and confuse simple choices about consumption for freedoms related to deeper, spiritual values.

A final aspect of freedom has to do with grounding our understanding of freedom in more universal terms. Fake freedom has to do with being concerned with my freedom only.

President Franklin Roosevelt reminded our nation about the importance of freedom in his 1941 speech to Congress, which he delivered nearly a year before the United States entry into the Second World War. In that speech, Roosevelt outlined what he considers to be four universal freedoms: freedom of speech and expression, freedom of worship, freedom from want, and freedom from fear.[4]

Roosevelt believed that each of these freedoms represented a universal, global right that connected us as nations. At the time, his speech was clearly addressing our nation's growing concern about fascism and Nazism in Europe. Roosevelt understood that societies can expand or narrow what freedom looks like beyond their own borders. And because freedom is a universal value that touches people in every nation, what affects one country can impact many others. This is certainly true in matters of war and peace, when people are displaced and armies violate national boundaries. We have also seen our interconnections and their impact on our universal freedoms

---

4. President Franklin Roosevelt outlined the Four Freedoms in his January 6, 1941 State of the Union speech. https://www.fdrlibrary.org/four-freedoms.

as we attempt to work globally on matters of pandemics and climate change. International relationships and personal freedoms are intertwined.

The universal beliefs related to freedom were of such importance that following World War II, nations gathered in the newly formed United Nations and adopted the Universal Declaration of Human Rights (UDHR) as a General Assembly in 1948. This declaration included many of the freedoms we are familiar with in the United States Bill of Rights, but it also went well beyond what were seen as basic rights in the eighteenth century.

The UDHR, translated into over five hundred languages, includes not only statements related to the freedom of speech, thought, conscience, religion, and assembly, but also addresses matters related to freedom from fear, slavery, torture, and arbitrary arrest, while also proclaiming the right to the freedom of movement, marriage, recognition, asylum, work, rest, and leisure, among other things. These inherent freedoms are seen as inalienable rights to which all are entitled "without distinction of any kind, such as race, colour, sex, language, religion, political or other opinion, national or social origin, property, birth or other status."[5]

Freedom is important individually, but it always has social consequences. One may be personally bigoted, which in itself is a spiritual concern, but that does not give that person the right or freedom to express hate speech nor deny another person their own cultural identity or personhood. Individuals do not have the right nor freedom to express their unwanted sexual desires toward others in inappropriate ways. That isn't a proper expression of one's freedom. It is sexual harassment or abuse.

These universal beliefs related to freedom always mingle with the freedom of others, and that is why laws are put in place and why our social structures are important to the development of community. One person's sense of freedom cannot deny someone else their freedom.

Freedom isn't about getting or doing whatever I want. It is about something much more significant. Nelson Mandela, who experienced the denial of his own freedom in prison for many years in Apartheid South Africa, put things into context with these powerful words: " . . . to be free is not merely to cast off one's chains, but to live in a way that respects and enhances the freedom of others."[6] This is both the challenge and opportunity that comes with real freedom. It is why one's expression of freedom begins within and is expressed by way of the spirit.

5. United Nations, *Universal Declaration of Human Rights*, article 2.
6. Crwys-Williams, *In the Words of Nelson Mandela*, 44.

Spiritual exploration:

- Make a list of ways in which you are able to exercise your freedom. Now make a list of freedoms that you see others denied within society. What do these two lists teach you about your sense of freedom?

The Problem with Selfishness

When I was in college, Ayn Rand's books and philosophy were still popular among many. Over the years, her classic works *The Fountainhead* (1943) and *Atlas Shrugged* (1957) have gathered a cult-like following since their publication in the mid-twentieth century.

I am not among her admirers. When I first read Rand's *The Virtue of Selfishness* in college, I remember wondering why a work of philosophy that was so shallow in terms of spiritual understanding had become so popular to so many.

In her works, Rand expresses strong support for laissez-faire capitalism and what she called rational self-interest. She believed that ethical egoism (what she spoke about in terms of Objectivism) was of greater value than collectivism or seeking the common good among people and societies. A good society was made up of individuals expressing their own sense of self-interest, not a community of people coming together to work toward common goals. In Rand's words,

> Since there is no such entity as "the public," since the public is merely a number of individuals, the idea that "the public interest" supersedes private interests and rights can have but one meaning: that the interests and rights of some individuals take precedence over the interests and rights of others.[7]

In her framework, she did not see the social experiment as working toward some greater social good by way of conversation, listening, partnership, and mutuality. Instead, Rand fought for limits on government and had a strong resistance to collaborative efforts grounded in any sense of altruism or community spirit, which she dismissed as false and harmful.

The more damaging impact of this narrow framing of reality is that it undermines community discourse among parties and hampers openness to the natural give and take that is a part of human community. Rand's

7. Rand, *Virtue of Selfishness*, 88.

singlemindedness reflects the ongoing struggle of how broad one's perspective is able to expand in order to live in harmony with others. It is anchored in one's own self-interest rather than growing to include one's clan, tribe, nation, or ultimately the larger world.

This struggle regarding where on the individual-to-community spectrum one anchors one's social framework is nothing new. It has taken many forms over the years from ancient tribalism to current nationalisms.

It was at the heart of Jesus' challenge to Roman rule that governed through proxy loyalties and Jewish tribalism's dismissal of those outside the tribe. Can one frame reality to include the non-Roman citizen and the Gentile? This was at the essence of Jesus' challenge to Roman and Jewish authority.

In self-centered frames and even nationalist ones, those who challenge these more self-centered perspectives are seen as dangerous individuals or agitators because they force the conversation to go beyond self-interest or the comforts of tribe. As we see in Jesus' case, his open-heartedness was punishable by death.

In our modern world, this danger is expressed in the threat to the established order that is embodied in movements for equality and equity for those who stand outside the corridors of power.

Upon reflection, Rand's brand of social philosophy, which still undergirds the prevailing American social movements of libertarianism and the "America First" perspective, is stuck in the early stages of spiritual development that James Fowler discusses in his work on faith development. It simply is unable to take into account someone else's view of the world. This limits our collective capacity to have a conversation or heal our social wounds. Compassion and empathy have to do with coming alongside someone else in order to be present with them. When I am frozen in my own self-centeredness, it is hard to develop these spiritual qualities because I am always wondering, "What's in this for me?"

There is a point in the adolescent phase of spiritual development in which one necessarily goes through what Jung and others describe as individuation (i.e., self-identity). This makes sense because, as we first develop, it is important for us to find our own self-identity in relationship to the world.

But as we develop more fully spiritually, it is important to learn how to integrate individuation within a larger understanding of the world: Who am I in relationship to you? What makes me different, unique, and similar to others? What am I uniquely called to be and do with my life? These questions must be responded to in terms of one's context and social relationships, not in isolation from others.

If one stays in the adolescent phase of development and fails to move beyond personal perspective and experience, spiritual development gets stuck here. If this happens, individuation becomes individualism and self-centeredness. Everything is then seen through a personal lens rather than extending ourselves to the complexities involved in human and social dynamics. One's preoccupation is with the question "How can I benefit?" rather than "What can I contribute?"

Beginning with these different questions leads to the formation of very different social relationships and communal understandings. One is oriented toward self-interest, the other toward community well-being.

The problems associated with the coronavirus reality challenge a purely self-interested approach to things: Can our collective welfare be adequately protected if I don't have some level of concern for your health and well-being? Am I as concerned about my responsibility to not spread disease as I am about yours? A pandemic has a way of reminding all of us that we actually need and depend on each other at a very real level. What is true of a pandemic is also true in regard to many other things, from having clean water or safe roads and highways to addressing matters of climate change.

Spirituality is always relational in nature, so it cannot end simply on personal, self-centered terms alone. We are a part of something much bigger than ourselves.

In his classic work, *Stages of Faith*, James Fowler writes about how we grow in faith over time and by interacting more deeply in the world. As he says: "Whenever we properly speak of faith it involves people's shaping or testing their lives' defining directions and relationships with others in accordance with coordinates of value and power recognized as ultimate."[8] This requires us to move beyond the early stages of adolescent spirituality so that individuation is a part of the movement toward spiritual wholeness rather than becoming the end point. If it is the goal, selfishness and even narcissism will be the natural result.

I've thought about this a lot during the unfolding of the coronavirus outbreak and the protests against institutional racism and police violence that have followed George Floyd's murder, since I was writing this book in the midst of those crises. Responding to these situations in a self-centered manner would be disastrous. On the one hand, in terms of the pandemic,

8. Fowler, *Stages of Faith*, 93.

everyone would be making decisions as if only their personal health and well-being mattered. In terms of racism, it would mean that this is someone else's problem to deal with, unless I am the person affected by racism myself.

Self-centeredness leads to an incomplete and unhelpful set of questions. Who has the authority or right to tell me I can't attend a community event if I decide that I want to do that based on my personal, rational self-interest? I don't feel like I'm a racist, so who are you to tell me that I am? The problem is that, on the one hand, my personal decisions could have deadly consequences for others, and on the other hand, if I am a part of the dominant culture, I benefit from an unfair system that gives me rights and privileges that others don't have. In both cases, my limited view of the situation is incomplete and fails to take into account the lives of others.

These diseases—both COVID-19 and racism—don't spread based on rational thought. They simply spread. You can't quarantine them behind walls or borders and assume that they will go away. In this sense, the working out of freedom and even one's own interest happen within a community context, which is always the case, even when we are not facing a pandemic or an institutional disease.

The world and even nature itself do not function in an isolated, compartmentalized manner. What affects one affects many, whether it is the result of a pandemic virus or expressions of hate or bigotry. While we do need to find our individual bearings in life, we are a part of communities and contexts that need to be understood and navigated collectively. All voices matter. There is such a thing as the common good. When we are in conversation with others, we are more likely to find a healthy equilibrium that honors our differences and is grounded spiritually.

Spiritual exploration:

- What is one selfish pleasure that is important to you that you could discuss with those involved in order to get their insights and perspectives on it?

Media and Technology

Another contextual reality that cannot be overlooked has to do with the pervasiveness of media and technology in our lives. Both of these social forces impact our sense of spirituality in significant ways. While they have clear social/relational qualities, they also speed up our sense of time, increase the flow of information, and alter how we interact as human beings with one another.

A lot has been written about the changes that technology is having on how we interact as individuals within society. Cyber bullying, violent video games, and online pornography have been especially called out as concerns that impact how we function. More recently, cyber attacks and computer hacking have raised important concerns that go beyond individual human interactions and encompass our ability to function as a democratic social order. Changes in technology and the use of social media affect our material as well as the spiritual realities.

Often, in today's setting, we notice technology's benefits without addressing or reflecting on the costs. In the march of progress, technology ends up reigning supreme even as some of the qualities that define humanity in spiritual terms get lost in the shuffle.

Jacques Ellul began addressing some of the spiritual implications of technology years ago, believing that there are a number of unforeseen consequences to our so-called technological progress. Ellul believed that we needed to take a closer look at the factors involved in technological advances because they have both benefits and costs associated with them.

In his book, *The Technological Bluff*, Ellul put it this way: "Human memory and foresight differ from those of computers. They include memories of joys and successes and failures, and the foresight is mingled with hopes and fears."[9] He goes on to say that

> intelligence is more than the ability to assemble and use knowledge to solve problems or to memorize. Intelligence is a total human activity. It is nourished by human relations, by accidents, by fatigue, by joy, by the desire to write or to calculate, by the selection of knowledge for a particular project, by psychological obsessions, by the wish to please or hurt people. The intellect is not algebra.[10]

What Ellul points to could be said in relationship to the human soul and spiritual life as well. Social media, in its many forms, has become a prominent way in which technology intersects with our spirits, both personally and socially. Increasingly, we have become dependent on social media to help us communicate with each other and even try to build community among us in new and different ways. When social media is used in irresponsible ways, from the promotion of false realities to personal attacks

9. Ellul, *Technological Bluff*, 163.
10. Ellul, *Technological Bluff*, 166.

on individuals among other things, communication, community, and spirit are all damaged, sometimes in irreparable ways.

This is not intended to be a blanket indictment of technology or social media. Both provide us with many remarkable benefits related to knowledge and understanding, comfort and social progress, cross-cultural insight and human knowledge. But other than bemoaning some of the significant concerns that technology and media create, we have tended to avoid addressing the consequences of technology in a deeper, spiritual manner. Much like our *carte blanche* acceptance of the marketplace culture, we ignore these realities at our peril.

Authors, such as Tal Brooke (*Virtual Gods*), Neil Postman (*Technopoly*) and others, remind us that technology is not value free. If we work to create an inward-out movement of the spirit that encompasses centering, framing, practicing, and living with others in healthy ways, we need to spend more time considering how technology and social media inform our journey without damaging our spirits or hampering our ability to create genuine community.

It is clear that technology will continue to shape and influence our culture. It is also clear that we will continue to rely on social media as a means of communication and connection. The question is: How will we bring our spiritual lives to bare on this emerging reality?

Spiritual exploration:

- What is one thing you could do with social media or technology to deepen human relationships in your life?

Cultural Gods: Holidays and Holy Places

Finally, there is one other barrier that impacts the overall health and wholeness of our spiritual journey. It has to do with the cultural gods we have created for ourselves as a society. Again, much like technology and social media, we are aware of this social dynamic but have not done much to address it from a spiritual vantage point.

As we look at our current context, it doesn't take much effort to see that there is a significant focus and preoccupation with celebrity culture within American society—what are the rich and famous doing in their lives? Many of them serve not only as cultural icons, but also as mentors for the young. In some cases, this adoration may be warranted, but in other cases, celebrities can abuse their fame and serve as poor role models.

When we step back from the influences of pop culture, who are the role models that we turn to regarding the spiritual principles that guide life? What can we learn from them regarding healthy wholeness?

In addition, our largest public settings, what one might call our "modern cathedrals," are not for the most part religious or sacred spaces. Instead, they are more often sports stadiums and arenas, shopping malls, and commercial structures that reflect the values of a marketplace culture. These are the edifices that are the largest and grandest in our society.

Years ago, many of our sports facilities had names such as Civic Stadium or Memorial Park. They now all have commercial names attached to them, as businesses use these modern cathedrals for advertising purposes.

What does it mean that we gather at places such as Little Caesar Arena (Detroit), KFC Yum! Center (Louisville), Smoothie King Center (New Orleans), Taco Bell Arena (Boise), or Sleep Train Arena (Sacramento)?

One might conclude that it really doesn't matter all that much. But the spiritual concern is this: What does it mean that our most significant community gathering places are an extension of the marketplace culture and represent a form of advertising rather than sacred space? Is there a difference between going to Grace Cathedral or a public park called The Commons as opposed to showing up at the Smoothie King Center or Taco Bell Arena? Does this difference impact our spirits in any way? I believe it does because we have lost an important sense of our collective identity and sacrificed it to commercial purposes.

We will never return to a non-commercialized version of these spaces, but the spiritual concern is this: When and where do we acknowledge public space and community gatherings in ways that connect us with deeper spiritual values related to wonder, awe, compassion, and justice?

This leads us to one other aspect of how our society loses its sense of soul to commercial values, which has to do with the celebration of many of our national holidays, what some societies consider "holy days."

In religious traditions, there are times set aside to help tell the story of a faith or are designated as times for personal spiritual renewal. Since we live in a society made up of a variety of religious traditions, there will always be a wide variety of such special occasions. As a society, we also lift up holidays in particular ways. How do we express the values and meanings we collectively attach to them?

Take, for example, the traditional American holiday of Thanksgiving. While in recent years, it has been the subject of much discussion related to the sensibilities about our national history and the treatment of Native Americans, it has also had a long history of being a family time focused on sharing our blessings as we come together to celebrate the fall harvest. Few remember that Thanksgiving's history stems from a proclamation that President Abraham Lincoln originally declared at the height of the American Civil War, making it a national holiday to remember the blessings and sacrifices of a nation.

However, in recent years, our marketplace culture and its media messaging has dwarfed this former American tradition with the trappings of sales and bargains associated with the creation of Black Friday. Now the values of good deals and shopping purchases dominate a season that was once about pausing to count our blessings and gather as families to share a meal.

Halloween, Mother's Day, and Christmas have long ago suffered from similar challenges from our culture's messaging. Halloween, which has roots in many forms across the world as a time to honor the passing of loved ones, has for many years in the United States been more about children collecting candy from neighbors rather than remembering those who have died. Mother's Days, which was originally created as a time to express love and appreciation for mothers, likewise has become so commercialized that it reflects more the values of the marketplace culture than it does its original intent.

On top of this, one commercial season just flows into the next as Christmas decorations go up right as Halloween candies come off the shelves. It is as if we are in a perpetual series of bargains and sales.

The spiritual question here is: What do these holidays and special times represent within our lives? How do we live out their original intent and values? Does it matter? And if not, are those prior values still important within our society?

Spiritual exploration:

- What could you do during an upcoming holiday to connect more deeply with its true meaning?

Conclusion

Each of these barriers impact our individual and collective spiritual lives. While I have addressed them from an American context, they all have a universal quality to them, since we are all impacted by a commercialized, global economy that maintains many of these traits. The question isn't, "Can we eliminate these cultural factors from society?" because they will not go away easily or willingly. Instead, the question is: "How can we nurture and nourish our spirits in ways that support and sustain the values most precious to us?"

We need ways to connect with the values associated with centering, framing, practicing, and living with others. Addressing racism, sexism, and homophobia, crossing class lines, identifying the real factors involved in freedom, coming to terms with technology and social media, and putting our cultural gods in their proper place are all an important part of rediscovering spirituality.

Who and what we notice about others says a lot about our sense of humanity. Our understanding of freedom foreshadows what we believe about living in community. How we utilize technology and social media reflects the value we place on relationships and our quest for knowledge and wisdom. How we celebrate and who we respect or idolize reflects the values we hold most dear. The issues involved with these barriers will not suddenly vanish, but we must discover and learn new ways to navigate them so they find their proper place in our lives.

8

Recovering the Spirit in Times of Political Peril

*Addressing Exceptionalism, Originalism,
Marketplace Culture, and Trumpism*

LET ME BEGIN WITH a personal story.

One morning, after our church's worship service, I noticed a young, Hispanic woman lingering in the narthex. She looked like she needed someone to talk to, so I approached her.

She was shy and did not speak English. I asked her, in my broken Spanish, how she was doing. It was clear that she needed attention, so I asked a laywoman in our congregation to join me so that the three of us could talk in my church office.

At one point in the conversation, I noticed that behind her long, dark hair, which covered one side of her face, she had what appeared to be a black eye. I asked her if she had been hit. She started to cry. It was clear she had experienced some kind of physical abuse, was experiencing fear, and was seeking help.

I asked her if it would be okay if I called our city's domestic violence hotline and connected her with a Spanish-speaking counselor. I did, and fairly quickly we got her situated in a safe house setting. The laywoman, who had helped me, and I felt like we had made a difference in this young woman's life, had done all we could, and were glad that such valuable resources existed in our city.

However, a couple weeks later, I received a call. It was from this young women's pro-bono attorney, who the domestic violence shelter had secured to represent her. The attorney asked the laywoman and me if we would be willing to appear in a courtroom on this Hispanic woman's behalf.

As it turned out, the lawyer explained that this young woman was undocumented, had a young son with a well-to-do Hispanic-American citizen, and that this man, the one who had abused her, had taken her to court in order to gain sole custody of the child and potentially have her deported to Mexico.

It was clear that this young woman was not just a victim of domestic violence, but that she also lived in fear of being deported and of losing her son. The woman's lawyer simply asked us to come to the courtroom, so that if the man took action against the abused woman that she would have someone present to stand up for her, let the judge know that she was a victim of domestic violence, and communicate that her partner should not get custody of their son.

As we sat in the courtroom, the man's attorney looked at us and then went to the front of the courtroom to talk with his client. I don't know what they discussed, but suddenly the two lawyers approached the bench and the case was dismissed. I'm not sure how everything worked out in the end, because I never saw any of them again.

But before I left the courthouse that day, I asked the young Hispanic woman why she came to our church that morning. She said something that has stayed with me ever since that time. She told me she looked out her kitchen window that morning down the hill from where she lived, she saw the cross on the top of our church building and said to herself, "Surely someone there can help me."

As it turned out, she was right. Our simple actions of noticing, listening, and responding made a world of difference in her life.

On one level, our actions were political and social in nature, but they started from a place within and worked their way out through ethically based social action. It didn't take much, but it did involve something that started in the spiritual realm first. What would happen in life and how might the world be different if we simply took the time needed to look at each other and realize that we need to be there for one another?

This interaction didn't really demand much from me, but it did require me to feel compassion, be curious enough to see what was really going on, and connect with another human being. In the process, I felt I was able to make a difference for someone else. In my life, I have experienced this very same kind of response and kindness from others as well.

At some point in our lives, we all need someone who is willing to walk with us through our struggles.

We need each other. This involves taking turns as we travel through the ups and downs of life. Even in the midst of our most troubling times, the spirit remains alive. But we have to pay attention and move from the physical to the spiritual realm in order for this to happen.

While spiritual life can be wounded and damaged, it cannot be permanently caged or controlled. Spirituality moves in too many diverse and independent ways for that ever to be true. It is why the spirit is always a threat to those with power, who want to have control. They not only are willing to deny others their freedom, but they are eager to confine resistance as well.

The challenge is that when the spirit is attacked in callous ways, how can we limit the harm done to individuals and the damage that impacts trust, gentleness, and understanding among us? This happens on both a micro, person-to-person level—as this story illustrates—and at a macro level, when social trends are set in motion. In both kinds of situations, we have the ability to influence our own fate.

If our spiritual lives continue to be out-of-order, our political life will never heal. We will not be able to experience true community as a people, let alone live up to the vision the American Founders articulated in the Declaration of Independence when they boldly proclaimed that all people are created equal and have a right to life, liberty, and the pursuit of happiness.

In 1789, our Founders created a constitution that itself became a sort of "peace pact" among the divergent and independent-minded states and individual religious practices. Through it, they sought to find enough common ground so that they could live in peace with one another. As Alan Taylor writes, "Those founders worried that their thirteen state republics, loosely tied in a new union, were vulnerable to internal divisions and external manipulation."[1]

The Founders' visionary, inclusive notion wasn't based on the idea that we, as Americans, are exceptional or unique, but instead that we are deeply human and naturally flawed. Because of this, they believed we need to put social mechanisms in place to check ambition, greed, and power. That is why the American experiment continues to be so bold politically. It assumes that we can create governmental structures capable of restraining

1. Taylor, "Virtue of an Educated Voter," line 9.

our human flaws. This is only possible if we not only honor the checks and balances that are a part of political structures, but if we are able to reorient ourselves spiritually so we see things in a more wholistic manner regarding collective life.

People like Washington, Jefferson, Hamilton, Adams, Franklin, and Madison saw the shadow of darkness in their own spirits clearly enough to realize that they had to create a government capable of preventing the impulse toward tyranny, monarchy, and oppression, even as some of them enslaved people themselves, didn't always get along with each other, and allowed Native peoples to be oppressed by the white newcomers to the land. The Founders got a lot of things right, but not everything.

They failed on the issue of equality for all when they didn't address and abolish slavery. They had a limited understanding of what "all" meant when they created a white, male property-owning class of leaders. This original flaw still haunts us today. As individuals, they were not on the same page in terms of the kind of society they wanted to create a great deal of the time. Yet they were ahead of their times in many ways, even though they were also men of their times.

Perhaps because so many of them had family histories of fleeing from narrow, restrictive, sectarian societies in Europe, they were able to piece together a loosely framed moral, spiritual understanding that gave them enough grace and understanding to see the importance of those universal human qualities they shared in common. As a result, they were able to create a democratic republic. Today, the United States remains a great experiment in social living.

Some of the Founders' assumptions were clearly faulty and need to be updated now. It is time to reexamine the spiritual underpinnings of life in our new, complex global setting so that we can return to our spiritual senses collectively.

In the beginning, the United States was a group of varied and disparate states that decided in the form of the Constitution to come together to create not just a federation of states, but to create a constitutional republic. It took their second effort to finally achieve the right mixture of form and structure that worked for all involved, since the first attempt, the Articles of Confederation, proved to be inadequate for the task.

Over time, this federation of different states formed more closely into something called a union—one nation. This union has been preserved over time, even as it has benefited some, while others have not experienced the fullness of the promises upon which it was founded.

In the twentieth century, when the United States joined together on the world stage to fight with our global allies during World War II, we found a way to protect the values that are at the heart of the American spirit. At the same time, we helped to prevent world domination by dictatorial, spiritless leaders, who had no qualms about tearing apart the social fabric of our common humanity or destroying any vestige of spiritual understanding between people.

In recent years, our efforts at social and civil union have quickly unraveled along the same fault lines that have been a part of the American experiment from the very beginning, including civil rights, racism, equality, and what it means to pursue happiness as individuals. This should not be entirely surprising since, as Colin Woodard articulates in his book, *American Nations: A History of the Eleven Rival Regional Cultures of North America*: "All of these centuries-old cultures are still with us today, and have spread their people, ideas, and influence across mutually exclusive bands of the continent. There isn't and never has been one America, but rather several Americas."[2]

In the past, this was mitigated in part through an American form of civil religion that gave enough space for each person and regional identity to function, while holding fast to some basic, common spiritual tenets that helped us maintain enough unity to survive together.

This is not to say that there was justice and fairness for all throughout our national history. This is clearly not the case. It is also true that different regions of the country have not honored the universal principles of justice and fairness equally. This has been a part of our national reality throughout our history. But more times than not, in spite of our differences, things held together under a semblance of unity and civility.

How was this possible? One answer comes from the 1830s, when Alexis de Tocqueville came to America and witnessed the remarkable American social experiment and saw something then that appears to be missing from our national landscape today. In Tocqueville's words,

> the character of the Anglo-American civilization . . . is the product . . . of two perfectly distinct elements that elsewhere have often made war with each other, but which, in America, they have succeeded

2. Woodard, *American Nations*, 2.

in incorporating into one another and combining marvelously. I mean to speak of the *spirit of religion* and the *spirit of freedom*.[3]

I believe in today's language, this could be expressed as the necessary balance that needs to exist between the spiritual and political realms in order for a society to be at peace with itself.

Tocqueville goes on to say, "I am of the opinion that absolute perfection is rarely to be found in any system of laws." Instead, he believed that public morality and the common sense of the people served as critical elements in making our political and social reality democratic and comparatively harmonious.[4]

We currently face the truth of this 1830 observation, and unless we reexamine our spiritual lives, individually and collectively, we will either attempt to legislate our way to conformity, which generally leads to repression and violence, or continue down our current path, which is marked by random acts of hatred and aggression perpetrated against one another in increasingly disturbing ways. We must find another way forward that probes our spiritual lives, but mediates our public, political lives.

In his recent book, *The Soul of America*, Jon Meacham says,

> Progress in American life . . . has been slow, painful, bloody, and tragic. Across too many generations, women, African Americans, immigrants, and others have been denied the full promise of Thomas Jefferson's Declaration of Independence. Yet the journey has gone on, and proceeds even now.[5]

Today, we have returned to our former state of disunity and separateness, believing different core values, following differing paths, and not willingly tolerating those who see the world differently. We have been here before, and in 1968, Robert F. Kennedy reminded us of what was needed for us to change direction when he said these words following the assassination of Martin Luther King Jr.:

> What we need in the United States is not division. What we need in the United States is not hatred. What we need in the United States is not violence and lawlessness, but is love, and wisdom, and compassion toward one another, and a feeling of justice toward those who still suffer within our country, whether they be white

3. Tocqueville, *Democracy in America*, 1.45.

4. Tocqueville, *Democracy in America*, 1.15.

5. Meacham, *Soul of America*, 5.

or whether they be black . . . Let's dedicate ourselves to what the Greeks wrote so many years ago: "to tame the savageness of man and make gentle the life of this world." Let us dedicate ourselves to that, and say a prayer for our country and for our people.[6]

The American experiment was, and still is, one of the great social experiments in human history, seeking to create a civic life capable of avoiding the excesses of aristocracy and unequal wealth, while also avoiding the pitfalls and chaos that results from rampant individualism and anarchy. If we are ever to get along politically, we will have to revisit fundamental spiritual foundations.

What is at stake? Nothing less than our collective future. In his address "The Quest for Peace," Howard Thurman expressed his concern about the fate of America by quoting an historian, who said: "The Roman Empire fell, not because of the failure of the hay crop, or because of any of the various economic interpretations of history. But the Roman Empire fell because the average Roman citizen lost a sense of personal responsibility for the fate of the empire." For Thurman, this concern applied to the United States as well, and the outcome involved our sense of spiritual life.[7]

Today, in spite of discouraging signs, we live in a world that continues to explore and travel in ways that to prior times would have seemed unimaginable. We are aware of so many different cultures today that not long ago were simply discounted or ignored. Through advances in technology, we have access to an infinite amount of information right in the palm of our hands. The vast diversity of religious and spiritual traditions is available to us in ways that our ancestors could not have foreseen. These realities allow the spirit to move freely.

Yet as we discussed in the last chapter, there are matters related to racism, class, freedom, technology, holidays, and public places that we need to be aware of in order for our spiritual lives to be well grounded.

In addition, there continues to be a gathering storm in the United States around several matters that jeopardize our spiritual life in fundamental ways, both as a country and as individuals who seek wholeness and harmony. Specifically, there are four current trends that when taken together harm our collective spiritual well-being.

6. MacAfee, *Gospel According to RFK*, 86. From Senator Kennedy's speech given in Indianapolis, Indiana on April 4, 1968.

7. Boeke, "Howard Thurman," 15.

These factors are exceptionalism, originalism, marketplace culture, and Trumpism. It is still unclear what the aftermath of the coronavirus pandemic will do to the material-spiritual equation and how it will become a factor in the future.

Each of these concerns raises a red flag that our spiritual selves need to pay attention to. When all of them are active together, as they are today, we should be deeply troubled and look for ways to address them appropriately from our spiritual centers.

Unfortunately, we have failed to address these growing concerns. Part of the issue has to do with the fact that we have focused our public attention on politics as if our current issues were simply about gaining power and winning political debates rather than create a system that encourages participation and social problem-solving among diverse people. Yes, politics and government are about laws and policies, but they are also about creating forums for discussion and wholistic decision-making that are open to all.

In addition, as a country, we have focused on the practices of religious institutions and how to maintain their survival rather than on how to encourage spiritual wholeness and develop a sense of openness toward different wisdom traditions.

The result of this misplaced attention is that smugness replaces hospitality, revenge replaces conversation and partnership, and political advantage focused on material outcomes replaces spiritual centering focused on ethical behaviors.

Let's explore these four key elements to see how they create the political brokenness that now afflicts us.

Exceptionalism

Exceptionalism has a long and varied history within the American view of itself. When this understanding concludes that the United States is unique and different from all other nations, because we are simply superior, we fall into a problematic spiritual abyss and create barriers to gaining spiritual maturity.

The notion that we are different in terms of creating a democratic system that has a unique, historic blend of checks and balances and other important democratic qualities is not a problem. After all, each nation has its own system of governance that is distinct and unique. However, to assume that this reality makes those of us in the United States different as human beings is simply not true and was not in the minds of the Founders who created our social structure to begin with. Jacob Needleman puts it like this: "Until we can free ourselves from the illusion of our moral uniqueness, our attempts to repair our crimes may never take us where we need to go."[8]

While Jefferson, Madison, Hamilton, and others held great hopes for what the United States might achieve and contribute to the world, they and their contemporaries were fully aware of the fragility of human beings toward matters of power, wealth, and ambition. For this reason, they designed a system in the United States to avoid the pitfalls of ordinary human life.

Today, the problem is that the idea of American exceptionalism has become a key element of our national myth that means we never truly analyze ourselves as a nation or criticize the decisions we make, because we are exceptional and can do no wrong. Exceptionalism, by its very nature, is declarative rather than being conversational, which means it is unable to interact or learn from others. When this happens, it becomes a kind of national idolatry and must be combated on a spiritual basis.

It is noble to be proud of our national heritage and to honor what the United States has contributed to world history. But it becomes a spiritual problem when we develop a sense of exceptionalism that denies the practice of the spiritual principles I've outlined in this book and simply assumes that all is well because America is different and can do no wrong.

In order to address this tendency, here are several things that we can do as individuals and as a society:

1. We can actively read about American history from a variety of points of view so that we get below the myth of exceptionalism and see the variety of competing narratives and storylines that give broader perspective to who we are as a people. We have shared our "better angels" on the world stage. We have also done the Devil's work in places as well. Reading history from different vantage points balances out our national story and grounds us in reality.

2. As individuals, we can have conversations with our neighbors who find themselves on the margins of society or who don't fit in the dominant culture's grand narrative. These individuals have something to say to us about what America means as well.

3. We can work in our communities and as a nation on the world stage to create alliances that acknowledge our common ground as human beings and countries, rather than decide that everything must be determined

8. Needleman, *American Soul*, 238.

on our terms alone. The old phrase, "America, love it or leave it" and "Make America Great Again" are simply not broad nor deep enough to gather us all in spiritually. Perhaps as things emerge in the post-coronavirus environment, we will be better able to do this globally.

Originalism

Originalism is a concept of law that interprets the American Constitution through a lens that believes this founding document should be interpreted only based on how it was originally understood by those who drafted it in the late 1700s. Other, more current historical factors remove it from its original intent. This stands in contrast to the notion that the Constitution is a living document whose legal principles should be understood in light of our current realities and times. This is an honest difference of legal opinion that has existed for many years.

In terms of spirituality, the problem with an originalist interpretation arises when things are seen through this lens and people's individual life circumstances are no longer taken fully into account because the law, as understood in the eighteenth century, cannot be challenged by these new or emerging realities. As a result, originalism denies us the ability to grow collectively. While exceptionalism declares uniqueness, originalism denies newness and changing context.

When this happens, the spirit is bound up in the law and how it was understood in a prior period of time that is not our own. Ultimately, this framing of life confines our current reality to rules of law rather than human realities. We've made an earlier understanding of law our God, so that it has become an end in itself rather than being a tool to serve the people in their present circumstances. At the same time, by validating an originalist approach to framing legal reality, we set up this model as being the dominant social norm since legal reasoning frames so much of our social and political behavior.

This way of thinking has impacted biblical interpretation as well. Is the Bible to be taken literally or is it a series of contextual documents, gathered over centuries in a variety of forms, that convey human understanding of God's intentions through the perceptions and voices of a number of authors, from the writers of Genesis to the Apostle Paul? Was the world created in seven days or do the insights of evolution have something to say to us about the created world in which we live? Does the Bible begin with Genesis and end with Revelation, or are Marcus Borg and others correct when they place the order the writing according to the scholarly research that dates each section? How you respond to these questions determines whether you look at the Bible as a complete, unchangeable work as determined by a series of early church council meetings and decisions or as a sacred document that invites us into a relationship with spiritual life and the discoveries that we uncover along the way.

It is easy to see why Galileo faced resistance and persecution in the early 1600s when he advanced Copernican thinking regarding the sun, not the earth, being the center of the universe. Through his work and evolving scientific research, our understanding of the world has changed. But in his own time, there were people in power who did not want their reality to change and resisted Galileo's evidence to the contrary.

This led to the Roman Church's inquisition of Galileo. At the time, officials within the church determined that what he was advocating was absurd. It was also contrary to scripture, making his philosophy heretical. For this, Galileo was arrested and placed under house arrest for the remainder of his life for introducing new information to previously understood certainties. This is always a danger when originalist thinking is taken to extremes.

While much of the debate about originalism occurs in courts of law and between professional judges and lawyers, there are several things that we can do as individuals and as a society to counter the negative dimensions of originalism:

1. Develop an understanding of the relationship of law and spirit within life. The give and take between these two understandings of the world is not new. The ancient Greeks and Hebrews, as well as societies in both the East and West, have long tried to determine the appropriate balance between the freedom of the spirit and the rule of law. Become familiar with some of these histories as you look at our current realities. Has the law always had the last word? When has it protected us from social chaos? When has the movement of the spirit freed us from the confines of earlier understandings that did more harm than good in the world? Know our collective history so we don't repeat the mistakes of the past.

2. Find locations in society in which people's lives are being harmed in real and lasting ways by a rigid focus on law, such as through current

immigration policies or some of our existing correctional system processes, and see how you can make your spiritual presence known in
these situations.

Marketplace Culture

We have referenced this concern a number of times throughout this book.
To be concerned about our growing marketplace culture is not to attack the
value of a market economy nor to criticize private enterprise as a means of
organizing the distribution of goods and services in society.

The problem of a marketplace culture arises when the centering social
narrative and myth of our country becomes a materialistic, selfish culture
in which things and people are not valued because of their sacred worth but
one-dimensionally because of their material and economic value.

When this happens, everything, including spirituality, becomes
compartmentalized within a materialistic framework rather than letting
things be seen as a part of a spiritual world. The consequences of such
an understanding are devastating to us as individuals and as a society.
They also have political ramifications, but the damage they do is first and
foremost spiritual.

This happens on multiple fronts, but let's focus on two principle concerns: (1) the effects of consumerism on us, and (2) what we end up paying
attention to and valuing.

In terms of consumerism, when a marketplace culture dominates our
society, we shift our focus to acquiring things and experiences rather than
building relationships and sharing our resources. In his book, *Consumed*,
Benjamin Barber says, "Selfishness no longer cloaks itself in religion: it has
become religion. Greed is not merely good for *me*. The new *ethos* wants
us to believe it *is* good in itself."[9] A marketplace culture needs to absorb
everything around it so that everything fits into the system and is given a
material value.

This has a significant impact on how we see, what we value, and how
we spend our time with each other. As the marketplace moves to com-
modify everything, we often end up doing this to each other as well. What
can you do for me? What is my time worth to you? Are you valuable?

---

9. Barber, *Consumed*, 47.

It is just a short step from here to not treating others as fellow human beings with kindness, dignity, and respect. Those who do the hard work of picking our food, making our clothes, caring for children and the elderly, and building our homes become invisible and expendable to us rather than being valued as craftspeople and workers who deserve to be treated fairly. The list becomes endless once we replace sacred worth with utilitarian value as our criteria, and this is a spiritual as well as an economic problem.

Here are a few simple things we can do to change this narrative:

1. During the upcoming holidays, consider ways in which you and your family can experience some of the celebration in spiritual ways.

2. Take time to interact relationally with those with whom you have an economic, transactional encounter. Is there an appropriate way to notice and thank those who help make your day better because of a service they provide to you?

Trumpism

Since 2016, we have seen the rise of what the media now calls "Trumpism." It is a social phenomenon that reflects the attitudes, practices, and behaviors of President Donald Trump, but it is about much more than the actions of one individual. It is about a way of thinking and behaving in society. While I disagree with much of Donald Trump's politics and many of his policies, my biggest concern has to do with the damage that Trumpism is doing to our spiritual lives.

Trumpism is based on confrontation rather than conversation, revenge rather than partnership, fear rather than hope, blame rather than inspiration. It is a scorched-earth approach to human interaction and relationships. It consistently takes traditions and icons of our American history and either distorts or diminishes their value by dislodging them from their prior history and meaning. Trumpism is grounded on a ruler-based understanding of governance. Rulers talk and make pronouncements; leaders listen and build partnerships.

By its very nature, Trumpism attacks. If you don't support me, you are against me. If you don't agree with me, you must be "human scum." If you are a stranger, you deserve hostility rather than hospitality. Tweets replace dialogue and campaign speeches replace community gatherings. None of these things require direct encounter nor social interaction between human beings. All of them tend to focus on the negative from a self-centered point of view. The spiritual world, which is based on abundance, blessing, and variety, is replaced with a purely physical understanding focused on scarcity, blame, and otherness. "Be awake and aware" becomes "Be afraid and suspicious."

Trumpism undercuts the basic principles of a spiritual life related to centering, framing, practicing, and living with others and moves everything into a political confrontation rather than seeing life as sacred and connected. As a result, Trumpism leaves a lasting stain of cynicism in the public sphere that is harmful to community-building and damages the sense that people can and do have a desire to practice good and serve others.

Those focusing on Trumpism politically have expressed concern about dictatorial ways and a lack of respect for the rule of law. Those concerned about the mental health that undergirds it point toward narcissism and self-centeredness. But if we are to rediscover the spirit in our current context, then we will need to address a more concerning spiritual dynamic—Trumpism is not self-reflective and is unwilling to admit wrongdoing or error. Spiritually speaking, when this is the situation, you have become your own God.

Those most supportive of President Trump's combative style like to refer to him as the "Disruptor-in-Chief." While it is clear that Trump is good at disrupting many of our political and social conventions, what is most worrisome is that in the process he is wreaking havoc on our spiritual lives.

Trumpism focuses our collective attention on incomplete and inadequate measures of greatness that have both personal and social aspects. Greatness isn't determined solely by stock market highs nor by successfully embarrassing one's supposed enemies through vicious tweets to the cheers of admirers. Such measures hold greatness too carelessly.

Instead, greatness has to do with the level of happiness that people feel in their lives, the sacrifices they are willing to make for the common good. Greatness has to do with the sense of partnership that develops within a society and the reality of justice that people experience.

The basic traits of Trumpism reflect a significant assault on all things spiritual and ultimately diminish the value of the human spirit. This is true even if they have become an effective political technique that others want to emulate.

The growing danger is that because this approach works so well politically, these attitudes and techniques have metastasized like a cancer throughout our body politic and have become a growing illness within our inner lives. Even those who are a part of Trumpism directly have been affected by its impact on society.

Trumpism, while appearing to be something new in our current context, has been with us in different forms throughout our history. There have been other proponents of the qualities it embodies from Strom Thurmond and George Wallace to Joseph McCarthy and now Donald Trump. We have confronted these dynamics before, but today we ignore Trumpism's spiritual impact at both our personal and social peril.

What can we do to combat Trumpism and remain spiritually whole?

1. Because of the toxic spiritual quality of Trumpism, sometimes it is important to simply disconnect from the news that surrounds us from time to time. This does not mean to ignore Trumpism or fail to respond to it in constructive ways. It simply means that Trumpism, because of the damage it does to the soul, requires us to disengage in appropriate ways. We need time to regroup within our inner lives before moving ahead. It is important not to respond to Trumpism in a Trump-like manner.

2. Find ways to be in connection and service to those who experience the greatest harm from Trumpism's attitudes and policies. This would include the immigrant and refugee communities, persons of color, those on the margins, people with disabilities, and others whose spirits are being attacked in today's political climate.

3. Create settings with others who have been afflicted with Trumpism in which you can create a conversation that is based on dialogue and questions rather than on a back and forth of pronouncements of differing opinions. This is not an easy thing to do and requires a great deal of spiritual preparation so that the interaction moves those involved closer together rather than farther apart. As hard as this is to do, we will not be able to heal our differences if this is not possible.

These four factors all play a role in how we frame our society today, and they impact how we function as individuals. If we are to find our way forward spiritually, we simply must understand the influences of these phenomena and find ways to counteract them in constructive ways. This means understanding the places from which they arise spiritually and practicing the spiritual principles that will change our world.

Wanting to be exceptional as a people is a positive trait. We should encourage that. But when we make our nation into an idol, we damage our soul.

Valuing the original intent of the Founders in creating the Constitution is a connectional commitment that holds us together as a country. But believing that the Founders eighteenth-century perspective is the be-all and end-all of how to understand our current context simply freezes our spiritual growth and social understanding. We are no longer living in a pre-iPhone, pre-sexual revolution, pre-culturally diverse world. Believing that we do only hampers our ability to find common ground with one another and leads us toward continuing division and conflict.

The marketplace adds great value to our ability to function as a society. But if we limit ourselves to an economically based valuation of each other, we miss many of the significant aspects of what human happiness is all about.

Trumpism reflects our deep yearning to be great, important, respected, and taken seriously by others. It reflects a yearning that many individuals express, who feel they have been neglected by the changes in society. These qualities are not bad qualities in themselves. But when they are used as a weapon to disempower or offend others or are taken out of social context and seen as pronouncements rather than conversations, they are elitist, confrontational, and socially damaging.

When these four qualities are combined, they become a spiritual Molotov cocktail, which is explosive and destructive. Exceptionalism can easily lead to arrogance; originalism can become fixated on the past; the marketplace culture can easily become overly utilitarian; and Trumpism often leads to cynicism in collective endeavors. When they become a part of our social framework, they undermine conversation, community, and ultimately social spirituality.

If we are to rediscover our basic spiritual nature and practice the spiritual principles outlined in this book, we will need to become fully aware of the dynamics and forces that challenge us today. The spiritual reservoir is deep and plentiful, but changing our political world and spiritual lives will take a significant amount of awareness, work, and practice.

9

Dealing with Conflict

Coming Together When Things Are Falling Apart

Good conversation connects us at a deeper level. As we share our different human experiences, we rediscover a sense of unity. We remember we are part of a greater whole.

—MARGARET WHEATLEY[1]

As WE HAVE SEEN in the two prior chapters, there are a number of barriers that stand in the way of collective harmony. Some of them are more universal in nature, while others are uniquely American.

Getting along with each other is not always easy. Sometimes there will be conflicts between us. We don't need to have a major argument in order to feel a sense of distance or alienation from others. Sometimes division takes place simply as a result of not seeing things in the same way. This should not be surprising. It is a normal part of human activity. However, division can also serve as a corrective and needed ingredient so that all parties involved can grow and become more spiritually whole.

As we experience the spiritual qualities of centering, framing, and practicing and move on to living with others, we notice that those around us have developed their own viewpoints, commitments, and sense of integrity. They do not view life in the same manner that we do. If a conversation

1. Wheatley, *Turning to Once Another*, 28.

ensues under such circumstances, it is likely to lead to a disagreement at some point. The question is: What happens between the people involved when this occurs?

Like many of the aspects we've examined in this book, dealing with conflict is an age-old issue. Countless social thinkers from political philosophers to management consultants have written on the subject. Others have weighed in with their own experientially-based wisdom about how to work through disagreements.

Over the years, we have received a variety of forms of advice from "Let's just agree to disagree" and "Count to ten before responding" to the elaborate processes involved in negotiating formal settlements or contracts, which include binding and legal obligations.

In their classic work, *Getting to Yes: Negotiating Agreement Without Giving In*, Roger Fisher and William Ury from the Harvard Negotiation Project describe a process they call "principled negotiation."[2] This process involves separating the people from the problem; focusing on interests, not positions; generating a variety of possibilities before deciding what to do; and insisting that the result be based on some objective standard. This approach makes a lot of sense when you find yourself in a formal process of disagreement.

Fisher and Ury feel strongly that it is important to humanize the negotiation process " . . . to deal with people as human beings and with the problem on its merits."[3] This is important because the goal is to get to "yes" together. In their words,

> In most instances to ask a negotiator, "Who's winning?" is as inappropriate as to ask who's winning a marriage. If you ask that question about your marriage, you have already lost the most important negotiation—the one about what kind of game to play, about the way you deal with each other and your shared and differing interests.[4]

Years ago, when I worked for Catholic Social Services in the San Francisco Bay Area, there was a period of time in which I served as the shop steward for the Service Employees International Union (SEIU) in one county where I was an employee while serving as an Interim Executive Director of the organization in another area. It was a strange situation to be

2. Fisher and Ury, *Getting to Yes*, 11

3. Fisher and Ury, *Getting to Yes*, 40.

4. Fisher and Ury, *Getting to Yes*, 154.

in, especially since during the prior contract year, the county where I was the shop steward had been involved in a difficult contract negotiation that had to be mediated by an outside resource. Negotiating a union contract can often lead to a time of tension within an organization for both union employees and management.

What I learned when I was involved in these two different contract negotiations simultaneously—one as a union negotiator and the other as the Executive Director, negotiating on behalf of management—is that people are more willing and capable of working toward a common solution when everyone is entrusted with complete information, there is a mutual sense of respect by all parties involved, and those participating are actively working to shape a common solution. This does not always happen. When it does, better results follow.

I remember returning to the parent board organization for these county agencies following my work as the Interim Executive Director, after completing the contract negotiations with the union representatives earlier than expected. I was greeted by one board member, who said, "How did you do this so fast? You are a magician!"

I didn't feel that magic was involved in that situation at all, even though the organization was dealing with a difficult financial situation that involved layoffs. While we had many difficult decisions to make during those contract negotiations, as the head of management, I gave the employees all the financial statements, and together we created a new contract agreement. It included making some difficult layoffs and cutting back hours for others. The difference was that we reached "yes" together because everyone was included in the decision-making process. The final agreement was not imposed by one side or the other.

Many conflicts are not nearly so formal, but they can nonetheless result in hard feelings and division among those involved.

From a spiritual perspective, the challenge is to move from the quality of "living with others" alone, which can easily get us into a reactive mode, and return to the spiritual process of centering, framing, and practicing first. Taking this simple step back gives those involved the time and discipline needed to ground themselves, try to make sense of what they see when given new information, perspectives, and context, and make sure that their actions are in keeping with their fundamental spiritual practices and habits. This assumes a sense of having an even playing field, which is often not the case, but those with power can change this dynamic if they want to achieve different results.

When this is achieved, we naturally move from the formality of the negotiation and agreement process toward the spiritual qualities of listening, understanding, conversation, and reconciliation. Like all conflicts we've discussed in these pages, the goal is not to win, but to find common ground. It is never easy, but it is always worth the time and energy involved because this is how we move from political brokenness toward spiritual wholeness. It is how you reach the summit together.

Conflict arises when individuals see things differently. This will always be a part of life. The question is whether or not we develop the capacity to move together as far as we can go without either party losing their integrity or sense of identity. This is true whether we are talking about union/management negotiations or interpersonal understandings within a marriage or relationship. We do make the road by walking and that happens best by way of centering, framing, and practicing basic spiritual principles before figuring out how to relate to and live with others.

For Further Reflection and Study

- Consider a prior situation in which you were in conflict with someone. How did it end? Did you reach common ground? What could you have done differently to impact the ultimate outcome?

- Consider a current conflict situation. What would need to be involved in order for you to get to "yes"? How could you move as far as you possibly can together? What would this involve?

10

Vocation

Discovering Life's Calling

Don't ask what the world needs. Ask what makes you come alive, and go do it. Because what the world needs is people who have come alive.

—HOWARD THURMAN[1]

IN THE MATERIAL WORLD, we each have a calling or vocation of some kind. It's what we often refer to as a job or career. Most of us get paid to do it. But our callings in life involve other roles and responsibilities, as well: including being a parent, child, sibling, neighbor, friend, community volunteer, etc.

In the spiritual realm, our callings do not generally result in getting paid. These callings are about matters of the heart. Sometimes individuals, such as priests, pastors, and rabbis are blessed to be paid for their spiritual vocations, but more often than not, this is not the case. One does not need to be religious, attend seminary, or lead the life of a monk in order to have a calling. Feeling a sense of call is a foundational part of being human, because it has to do with responding to the question: Why am I here—and what am I called to do with my life?

I think about this in terms of doing my blessing journal every week for twenty-five years. For a long time, it was something I did, but at some

1. Quoted in Bailie, *Violence Unveiled*, xv.

point, this practice simply became a part of who I am as a person. Callings are like that. They are those things that aren't about something that you *do*, but something that you *are*.

In terms of the mountain climbing imagery we have been using, the climb and everything associated with it is something that we do, but the desire to reach the summit and the inspiration to climb in the first place comes from a sense of calling that dwells within the human spirit.

Let me illustrate it by this personal experience. When I was a local pastor at Portland First United Methodist Church, there were occasions when I had the opportunity to sit in the chancel area while an amazing violinist and member of the congregation, Rebecca Anderson, came forward to play a beautiful piece of music as an anthem or offertory.

At the time, she was a high school student. Since then, she has gone on to become an amazing concert artist. Rebecca is a truly gifted musician. When she played at our church as a young musician, I would be sitting up front just a few feet away.

On one occasion, Rebecca came forward to play, put her sheet music on the stand, closed her eyes, and proceeded to perform an exquisite piece of music that held the congregation breathless. She played without ever opening her eyes.

I know that most great musical talents are able to play without looking at their music, but watching Rebecca on that particular occasion years ago reminded me of how powerful it is to witness someone who is so linked to what they are doing that it flows out of them naturally, as if coming from someplace else. In this case, Rebecca and the music simply became one.

Callings are like that. They come from a place so deep inside that they aren't just something you do. They are something you become! Frederick Buechner frames it in this way: "[Your vocation in life] is the place where your deep gladness and the world's deep hunger meet."[2] True spiritual vocation takes place at the intersection of the personal and the social dimensions of life and transforms things in powerful ways.

We don't need to be great musicians or artists or dedicated athletes in order to live out our deepest sense of calling. All of us have something inside that helps us express our lives in profound ways. The challenge is to wait for, listen to, and respond fully to these inner urges, so that our lives become aligned with higher, transcendent purposes. This generally involves

2. Buechner, *Wishful Thinking*, 119.

centering, framing, and practicing without being conscious of these steps. One is simply in a natural flow of spiritual energy.

In order to uncover one's spiritual calling, you have to be asking the right life questions. It isn't so much about knowing what to do as it is about knowing who you are. We have been looking at what these questions are throughout this book, and they have to do with nurturing one's inner life and seeing how to give our "better angels" the space they need to take flight and engage the world in meaningful ways.

It isn't always about grand plans so much as it is about who one is at a given moment in time. Viktor Frankl put it like this: " . . . the meaning of life differs from (person) to (person), from day to day, and from hour to hour. What matters, therefore, is not the meaning of life in general but rather the specific meaning of a person's life at a given moment."[3]

But why does calling matter?

Calling matters because it relates to both of the human hungers (i.e., the physical and the spiritual) that are a vital part of daily life. If life were only about our physical hunger, we'd only be here to eat and stand in buffet lines. But life is about so much more than that. It is about creating a sense of compassion and community, gratitude and justice, kindness and harmony in our world and lives. We need to discover why we are here and then learn how to express this in tangible ways. E. Stanley Jones put it this way: "That which is to reach the heart must come from the heart. If the heart is empty, then deep does not speak to deep. Shallowness speaks to shallowness."[4]

Because calling is about heart matters, there is often a "before" and "after" quality to it. Life just isn't the same on the other side once a calling is discovered and claimed. It is also true that there are incremental qualities to this discovery as well, because, as Frankl indicates, there is a moment-to-moment quality to life when we are talking about deep meaning. We discover the depths of our calling as we travel through life, and this involves an endless string of specific encounters. It is not just about reaching a single summit in one's life, but about all the steps that have been taken along the way. In fact, once a summit has been reached, there is usually another summit off in the distance waiting for a future journey.

It is true that we need jobs that pay us enough so that we can eat and have a place to live in the material world, but we also need to uncover our spiritual calling so that we can activate what has the deepest meaning in our

3. Frankel, *Man's Search for Meaning,* 171.

4. Jones, *Way,* 272.

lives. This is the place where the inward-out movement finds expression. William Stafford, the great American poet, put it this way, "Your job is to find what the world is trying to be."[5]

As we have seen in earlier chapters, we live in complex times, which means that learning about life's meaning and our role within it can be challenging. Mary Catherine Bateson, in her book, *Composing a Life*, reminds us, especially women, that the search for composing life is not as clear or easy as it once was:

> Today, the materials and skills from which a life is composed are no longer clear. It is no longer possible to follow paths of previous generations. This is true for both men and women, but it is especially true for women, whose whole lives no longer need be dominated by the rhythms of procreation and the dependencies that these created, but who still must live with the discontinuities of female biology and still must balance conflicting demands. Our lives not only take new directions; they are subject to repeated redirection, partly because of the extension of our years of health and productivity. Just as the design of a building or of a vase must be rethought when the scale is changed, so much the design of lives. Many of the most basic concepts we use to construct a sense of self or the design of a life have changed their meanings: Work. Home. Love. Commitment.[6]

Navigating the spiritual dimensions of reality is especially critical today, because of the growing social imbalance that focuses our attention primarily on the material and political aspects of life. In order for this imbalance, and its resulting dysfunctions, to be addressed and resolved, we all need to spend time grounding ourselves in those yearnings and practices that will enable us to use our time on earth more wisely and that will help us participate in the healing of the world. In this sense, we are called to aid in the process of moving from political brokenness to spiritual wholeness.

Calling involves a natural movement from inside out, and it will happen when enough of us take up this challenge and come back to our spiritual centers long enough to discover our true spiritual callings.

5. Stafford, "Vocation," line 15.
6. Bateson, *Composing a Life*, 2.

For Further Reflection and Study

- What do you see as being your calling or vocation in life? One way to consider this would be to think about what you'd like people to say about you at the end of your life. What words would you like people to use? What would be your legacy?

- What do you do with your time that makes you feel most alive? How do you express this in the world?

- What title or titles would you give to what you do in life? Create a complete list. Which ones resonate most deeply in your spirit?

Epilogue

As a society, we remain at the critical crossroads I described earlier. This crossroads has become even more critical as the coronavirus and the protests following the murder of George Floyd and other unarmed African-Americans have left their imprint on our lives and collective consciousness. Both COVID-19 and a deeper understanding of the real impact that racism has on our common humanity have changed how we relate to one another and see our common life.

COVID-19 has already demonstrated that things will not be the same in the foreseeable future. It has exposed the divides—material, racial, economic, and ethical—that exist between us. In some cases, in recent months, they have even widened. To change things, we will need to behave directly in social settings.

The protests that followed George Floyd's murder by police officers have opened up the possibility to finally address our historic racism—on both personal and institutional levels—in ways that will require deep self-reflection, difficult conversations, and intentional institutional and legislative reform at all levels of society. We will need to rise to the occasion for this to happen.

In the United States, much of the twentieth-century was marked by the maintenance of a fragile political union based on compromised political accommodations, which turned a blind eye to racism, sexism, homophobia, and economic inequality among other things. This union was based on a kind of civil religion that presumed social niceness and civility, was held together by the Judeo-Christian ethic of "do unto others as you'd have them do unto you," and presumed a membership-based understanding of religious practice that lacked theological depth, critical conversation, and spiritual discipline. As a result, many of the injustices that are anathema to fundamental spirituality were allowed to continue as long as they weren't significantly challenged.

Beginning in the 1950s with the Civil Rights Movement and continuing through advocacy efforts related to women's rights, Native Americans, the farmworker community, the LGBTQ community, and moving through the #MeToo movement and the recent protests against police brutality toward people of color, this prior civil religion and tendency to conform socially has evaporated and been replaced by a state of political and spiritual brokenness that is alienating us from each other.

The question before us now is: As we stand at this crossroads, will we choose to do something bold and different that is capable of healing us as a nation and lead us toward spiritual wholeness or will we return to the way things were before and remain satisfied to continue our political division? The outcome is up to us.

I am a generally upbeat person, and while I remain hopeful that we can move from political brokenness to spiritual wholeness, based on current events, I am not necessarily optimistic that we will do so. The move from a materially based worldview to one that is spiritually grounded is clearly within our reach. The problem is that this movement will require a change in our consciousness. From my experience, this most often occurs when someone has an epiphany that alters their consciousness or when they go through a dark night of the soul (i.e., experience and work through some kind of tragedy or deep suffering). In the absence of such things, it is easy to just continue going about business as usual.

Commentators from George Will to E.J. Dione, scholars from Jon Meacham to Jacob Needleman, religious writers from Diana Butler Bass to those associated with Christian apocalyptic writing have all written about where they think we are headed as a society based on our situation during the past several years. Will we become more authoritarian or return to our democratic roots? Will the coming days lead to the end of the world, where only those who are pure enough are spared through divine intervention, or will this be a time of remarkable spiritual renewal for all? There are advocates for these and many other perspectives during this turbulent time.

Ultimately, if real social change is to take place, we will all need to be open to and include diverse insights and perspectives, as well as new voices, in the discussion, so that we can better understand ourselves and our neighbors. No one perspective is inclusive enough to capture all that needs to be said, which means that the dominant culture must learn to listen and be willing to give away some of its power and authority. The movement from political division to spiritual wholeness will not take place until an inclusive conversation occurs in earnest, where there is mutual respect and a willingness to listen to and learn from others.

I am a white, progressive, heterosexual, cisgender, middle-class person who happens to live on the West Coast, uses the pronouns he/him/his, and has Christianity as a key factor in my formational understanding of spirituality. While I have traveled a great deal internationally and worked in various cross-class and cross-cultural settings, I am an American and have lived much of my life near Portland, Oregon. There are other adjectives that could describe who I am, but the point is that I have a particular perspective that is influenced by a variety of traits, qualities, and privileges that impact what and how I see and experience things. My perspective is only one among many that need to be a part of the journey forward.

In *Rediscovering the Spirit*, I have attempted to describe the assets and challenges that I see before us as individuals who seek meaning in our lives and as an American society seeking to overcome our differences and divides. I also understand that in order for us to reach equilibrium personally and socially, and in order for us to learn how to modulate our spiritual energy with one another, we need to create open spaces for each of us to share what rediscovering the spirit means from our various, unique perspectives that are not white, middle class, progressive, heterosexual, American, Christian, or West Coast. We need to listen to and actually hear the voices of the many in order to become one.

Only when we are willing to covenant with each other to do this will we approach a sense of inner peace and social harmony. In the absence of creating such an atmosphere, we will not only fail to hear all the voices among us, regardless of culture or class, but also continue to "otherize" those who are not like us. It is easy not to listen to others; it takes effort and spiritual maturity to be open to those around us who may be different.

The essential questions of how to live together in the world are still before us. The choices we make—individually and collectively—in the near future will determine what our world will look like and how we will relate to one another for years to come. Those choices will inform our centering myths, determine our social and political frameworks, and influence how we treat each other. It is my hope that we will make the choices needed to move us from our ongoing political brokenness toward a place of spiritual wholeness.

In order for this to happen, it will be important for the quality of *equilibrium,* which we discussed in relationship to centering and framing, coalesce with the characteristic of *modulation,* which we described in the section on practice, in ways that lead toward spiritual wholeness and break through the pattern of political brokenness that has plagued us for far too long. Equilibrium is about inner balance. Modulation is about the appropriate use of spiritual energy.

How can we develop a sense of inner equilibrium so that the world becomes healthier and more whole as we ourselves become more balanced within? How do we create the capacity to modulate our spiritual energy for the greater, common good in ways that build connection and community? These are the critical questions that we must come to terms with for political brokenness to be overcome.

When this happens, the great challenges of racial injustice, economic inequality, health disparities, and environmental degradation can finally be addressed not from adversarial political positions, but from the common ground of spiritual insight and ancient wisdom. How do we address these matters in ways that honor our role as stewards of our time, without jeopardizing the future of those who will follow us on the trail of human history?

In the early twentieth century, Mohandas Gandhi did this in an inward-out manner that was based on *satyagraha* or "soul force." This word comes from a Sanskrit word that means "insistence on truth." Sanskrit is the liturgical language of Hinduism, and Gandhi employed this spiritual concept in a social manner that became non-violent resistance to British rule in India. Through the blending of the spiritual with the social, Gandhi deployed what he called "soul force" as a political tool to overcome an oppressive system and defeat colonialism. The power of *satyagraha* came from a deeply spiritual, disciplined place. It moved from the heart to become a physical force that Gandhi utilized effectively in the world.

In the 1950s and 60s, Martin Luther King Jr. redeployed the concepts that Gandhi introduced from within his tradition to a new context and situation to address social injustice in the United States. Today, we must find our own version of "soul force" to address the social context in which we live. This will require a deep search within, combined with a thoughtful analysis of the social conditions we face today. This is the essence of the inward-out movement.

In many ways, while this book took several months to write, I've been working and researching its content for over fifty years. In 1970, I wrote what I called "My Twelve Philosophies of Life to Live By" and posted them by my bedroom door to read before heading off for school each day. I was sixteen at the time and wanted to be conscientious of how I lived, including how I understood the divine/human encounter, what the inward journey involved, and how I wanted to live in the larger social context.

Lots has changed since then, but the kernels of what was reflected all those years ago are still a part of who I am and what I believe today. Those initial kernels of thought about the purpose and meaning of life and who I wanted to be had a lot to do with centering, framing, practicing, and living with others, even if I didn't have the ability to put it into so many words at the time. That early "philosophy of life" document also provided me with both a compass and a direction that consistently pointed toward seeking spiritual depth in my journey and the desire to seek connection and community with others. These instincts have served me well and made me feel very much alive—even in my darkest days. I did not know then that I was engaged in the mythic mountain climb that I have discussed in *Rediscovering the Spirit*, but that has indeed been the case.

Life and the ascent that is involved with it are not without significant hurdles that challenge one's journey. The course varies depending on the unique obstacles and opportunities that lie before each of us personally, as well as the larger, historical era that we find ourselves a part of. There will be, without a doubt, lost moments, miscarriages of justice, unwarranted prejudices, and sometimes even abuses that we must face along the way. There will also be open doors, serendipities, and blessings that lighten our travels.

On a social level, some will live in times of war, economic difficulty, racial injustice, even pandemics, while others will experience times of prosperity and peace. If history demonstrates anything, it is that more often than not this range of circumstances will fall upon a single lifetime.

While the political and material realms we deal with will frequently create a wide range of reactions and often result in division and acrimony, we have the ability to find common ground—and higher ground—that can unite our spirits and help us establish a common cause with one another.

Life is a spiritual odyssey, filled with blessings, celebrations, challenges, temptations, and distractions. When isolation, alienation, hopelessness, bitterness, and hatred get the upper hand over connection, community, love, empathy, and compassion, the result is a steady and incremental movement toward spiritual disarray and social division. This is what we are experiencing today.

It is possible, however, to reaffirm where the spirit is present in the world and rediscover the principles and practices that connect us more deeply to ourselves, our world, and one another. In her book, *Christianity after Religion*, Diana Butler Bass writes, "As the old gods (and the institutions that preached, preserved, and protected the old gods) lose credibility, people begin to cast about for new gods—and new stories, new paths, and new understandings to make sense of their new realities."[1]

We have seen this happen in new and disturbing ways as many people in the United States have returned to old (not new) forms of tribalism and nativism, hoping to put their personal and social worlds back in order. The problem is that many of these old paths are damaging our country since they are being framed into narrow ideological positions that have no deep spiritual grounding. This phenomenon in itself has led us to a precipice that may ultimately destroy our spiritual national heritage.

The journey, however, is about spiritual growth, not religious affiliation. When James Fowler wrote *Stages of Faith* years ago, he reached a similar conclusion:

> The issue is finally not whether we and our companions on this globe become Muslims, Jews, Buddhists, Taoists, Confucianists or Christians, as important as that issue is. The real question is, will there be *faith* on earth and will it be *good* faith—faith sufficiently inclusive so as to counter and transcend the destructive henotheistic idolatries of national, ethnic, racial and religious identifications and to bind us as a human community in covenantal trust and loyalty to each other and to the Ground of our Being?[2]

I don't believe that our various religious traditions are the only way in which spiritual grounding takes place in the world, but I do believe that our rich, religious, and cultural expressions of spirituality can and must play a role in reframing our future. Ultimately, it will be a blend of perspectives and understandings that will help us shape the future. This will require openness and a willingness to learn from those who come from different traditions and see the world in unique ways. It will also mean crossing our class and cultural divides.

Without a new, more universal sense of spiritual grounding, we will replay ancient hatreds and maintain old prejudices in ways that result in negative political consequences. Only when we return collectively to our

---

1. Bass, *Christianity after Religion*, 68.
2. Fowler, *Stages of Faith*, 293.

spiritual moorings will we find a way forward that moves through compassion and justice to a place of harmony and peace. It is an inward-out, spiritual-to-political path that all the great wisdom teachers understood.

We are the beneficiaries of great scientific advancement, but without spiritual principles to ground these discoveries, we are capable of great harm. At the same time, religious practices, without the insight and knowledge of modern science, can lead to antiquated ways and parochial understandings of the world that foster prejudice and hatred. We need to come to terms with both dynamics so that the material and spiritual worlds are each valued and respected.

At the same time, it is important to restate that while spirit matters, we will never reach our destination if we don't support laws that honor equality and justice. Without a fair, inclusive legal framework, those in power will suppress, confine, and damage the spiritual quality of a society. Those on the margins will be seen as essential, but treated as expendable.

Martin Luther King Jr. put it this way: "It may be true that the law cannot make a man love me, but it can keep him from lynching me, and I think that's pretty important."[3] Laws are the result of the spiritual battles that take place within us as a society. As we learned earlier, even a law against murder could not prevent James Earl Ray from killing Martin Luther King Jr. That battle was lost within his own spirit long before he decided to pull the trigger.

But laws matter and ultimately spring from within our collective soul. This is why the American Founders created a system of checks and balances to build a political system capable of harnessing those human impulses that damage the human spirit. It is why they were inspired to write the Declaration of Independence—written from the realm of spirit—while also laboring to create a political system that honored that spirit through checks and balances and the distribution of power (i.e., the US Constitution and Bill of Rights). The ultimate goal is to create a legal system that comes from deep within and makes room for our better angels to take flight.

After all the devastating violence and war of the twentieth century, Reinhold Niebuhr reminded us that the journey toward wholeness and civility is long and ongoing. In his words,

> Nothing that is worth doing can be achieved in our lifetime; therefore, we must be saved by hope. Nothing which is true or beautiful or good makes complete sense in any immediate context

3. King, *MLK at Western*, 14.

of history; therefore, we must be saved by faith. Nothing we do, however virtuous, can be accomplished alone; therefore, we are saved by love. No virtuous act is quite as virtuous from the standpoint of our friend or foe as it is from our standpoint. Therefore, we must be saved by the final form of love, which is forgiveness.[4]

In many ways, we have come full circle in this study of our times and returned to the threshold where the personal and the social meet and where the spirit and material co-mingle, giving birth to what matters most and binds us to each other.

There is an urgent need to explore new ways for new times. In the end, our mutual exploring can return us to holy ground and remind us that our journey is a sacred gift entrusted to each generation anew.

In 2019, when my wife, Susan, and I drove across the United States, we went through twenty-five states. We saw our great national heritage on full display from our national parks to countless historical sites and museums. We saw the good and bad of our nation's journey and heard stories that brought life to our rich cultural past.

We did not see red states and blue states, even though we traveled through them. We did not see walls nor experience hostility, though both were undoubtedly hidden in various ways from our view.

What we saw instead were people sharing their stories and bearing witness to what we can be at our best. There was rich, colorful diversity as well as regional uniqueness.

There is spirit alive among us, but it will take time to center down, reframe our expectations, listen more and talk less, practice what our "better angels" have to say, and reach out and decide to live with a focus on peace with justice toward one another. This will take work, but it is within our collective reach.

As the twenty-first century continues to unfold, we need to join hands with one another and commit ourselves to the important spiritual work that lies ahead. The spirit is alive, but things will not change until we acknowledge its power and use these inner resources to challenge ourselves and the world in which we live.

This is not the first time that our nation nor the world has found itself at a spiritual crossroads, but today is one of those critical moments. We are living at a time that requires us to recommit ourselves to spiritual basics as fellow citizens.

---

4. Niebuhr, *Irony of American History*, 63.

Epilogue

If we practice the spiritual disciplines of finding our center, framing our reality, practicing spiritual principles, and living with and engaging others in a spirit of wholeness, our personal and social worlds will reach a harmonious spiritual equilibrium. It is the confluence point of these characterstics working together among us that will change our consciousness and shift the momentum from political brokenness to spiritual wholeness.

In prior eras, when faced with times of threat and crisis from the outside, nations were known to rise up, declaring a "call to arms" in order to defend itself against external enemies. Perhaps, as we experience a threat to our very souls, it is time to proclaim a "call to hearts" so that we can rise up and preserve our spirits. We are living in such a time as this, and perhaps this call has already gone out.

One on level, when millions of people around the world viewed the video of George Floyd being murdered by a white police officer as other officers stood by and did nothing to stop it, they received such a "call to hearts." At that moment, we all realized that we cannot remain bystanders when such racial injustice and inhumanity takes place before our eyes. It is no longer a theoretical matter, but something quite real. Human life and our spirit is at stake. The question is: What will we do when we receive such a call?

We are now in the midst of a dramatic mountain climb. This venture will take us to both the heights of human experience as well as the depths of our being. We are involved in this venture together. I wish you well on the next steps in your travels. We will need each other throughout the journey. May you stay awake, be alert, remain safe, and find the path that ultimately leads you forward and helps us all reach the summit together.

Bibliography

Abdullah, Sharif. *Creating a World that Works for All*. San Francisco: Berrett-Koehler, 1999.

Alexander, Michelle. *The New Jim Crow: Mass Incarceration in the Age of Colorblindness*. New York: New, 2012.

Allison, Jay, and Dan Gediman, eds. *This I Believe: The Personal Philosophies of Remarkable Men and Women*. New York: Henry Holt, 2006.

"Americans gave $427.71 billion to charity in 2018 amid complex year for charitable giving." *Giving USA*, June 18, 2019. https://givingusa.org/giving-usa-2019-americans-gave-427-71-billion-to-charity-in-2018-amid-complex-year-for-charitable-giving/.

Armstrong, Karen. *Compassion: An Urgent Global Imperative*. Washington, DC: Brookings, 2012.

Artress, Lauren. *Walking a Sacred Path: Rediscovering the Labyrinth as a Spiritual Tool*. New York: Riverhead, 1995.

Bailie, Gil. *Violence Unveiled: Humanity at the Crossroads*. New York: Crossroad, 1996.

Barber, Benjamin R. *Consumed: How Markets Corrupt Children, Infantilize Adults, and Swallow Citizens Whole*. New York: W.W. Norton, 2007.

Bass, Diana Butler. *Christianity after Religion: The End of Church and the Birth of a New Spiritual Awakening*. New York: HarperCollins, 2012.

Bass, Dorothy C., ed. *Practicing Our Faith*. San Francisco: Jossey-Bass, 1997.

Bateson, Mary Catherine. *Composing a Life*. New York: Penguin, 1990.

Bellah, Robert N., et al. *The Good Society*. New York: Random House, 1992.

———. *Habits of the Heart*. New York: Harper and Row, 1985.

Benedict of Nursia. *The Rule of St. Benedict in English*. Edited by Timothy Fry. Collegeville, MI: Liturgical, 1982.

Berger, Peter. *The Sacred Canopy: Elements of a Sociological Theory of Religion*. New York: Doubleday, 1967.

Blakesley, Paul J. "Shock and Awe: A Widely Misunderstood Effect." Thesis, United States Army Command and General Staff College, 2004.

Boeke, Richard. "Howard Thurman: Black Mystic of San Francisco." *Creation Spirituality* (March/April 1991) 12–16.

Boyle, Gregory. *Tattoos on the Heart: The Power of Boundless Compassion*. New York: Free, 2010.

Brooks, David. *The Road to Character*. New York: Random House, 2015.

Bibliography

Brown, Brené. "Brené Brown's 6 favorite books that inspire bravery." *The Week,* October 27, 2017, https://theweek.com/articles/728875/bren-browns-6-favorite-books-that-inspire-bravery.

———. *Daring Greatly.* New York: Gotham, 2012.

Brussat, Frederic, and Mary Ann. *Spiritual Literacy: Reading the Sacred in Everyday Life.* New York: Scribner, 1996.

Buechner, Frederick. *Wishful Thinking: A Seeker's ABC.* San Francisco: HarperOne, 1993.

Campbell, Joseph, and Bill Moyers. *The Power of Myth.* New York: Anchor, 1991.

Canales, Jimena. *The Physicist and the Philosopher: Einstein, Bergson, and the Debate that Changed Our Understanding of Time.* Princeton, NJ: Princeton University Press, 2015.

Carlson, Richard, and Benjamin Shield, eds. *Handbook for the Soul.* Boston: Little, Brown and Co., 1995.

Carnegie, Andrew. *The "Gospel of Wealth" Essays and Other Writings.* New York: Penguin, 2006.

Cashman, Kevin. *The Pause Principle: Step Back to Lead Forward.* San Francisco: Berrett-Koehler, 2012.

Chapman, Gary. *The 5 Love Languages: The Secret to Love that Lasts.* Chicago: Northfield, 1995.

Charleston, Steven. *The Four Vision Quests of Jesus.* New York: Morehouse, 2015.

Chittister, Joan. *Called to Question: A Spiritual Memoir.* Lanham, MD: Sheed and Ward, 2004.

———. *Welcome to the Wisdom of the World and Its Meaning for You.* Grand Rapids: Eerdmans, 2007.

Chodron, Pema. *Comfortable with Uncertainty.* Boston: Shambhala, 2002.

Church, Forrest. *The American Creed: A Spiritual and Patriotic Primer: A Spiritual and Patriotic Primer.* New York: St. Martin's, 2002.

Cousineau, Phil. *The Art of Pilgrimage: The Seeker's Guide to Making Travel Sacred.* Boston: Conari, 1998.

Crwys-Williams, Jennifer, ed. *In the Words of Nelson Mandela.* Secaucus, NJ: Carol, 1998.

Dalai Lama and Desmond Tutu. *The Book of Joy.* New York: Avery, 2016.

Dawson, George, and Richard Glaubman. *Life Is So Good.* New York: Penguin, 2000.

Day, Dorothy. *The Long Loneliness: An Autobiography.* New York: Harper and Row, 1952.

de Botton, Alain. *The Art of Travel.* New York: Pantheon, 2002.

de Saint-Exupéry, Antoine. *The Little Prince.* Translated by Richard Howard. Boston: Mariner, 2000.

de Tocqueville, Alexis. *Democracy in America.* 2 vols. New York: Vintage, 1945.

Dickens, Charles. *The Christmas Carol.* Seattle: AmazonClassics, 2017.

Duhigg, Charles. *The Power of Habit.* New York: Random House, 2012.

Edelman, Marian Wright. *Guide My Feet.* Boston: Beacon, 1995.

Ellis, Catherine, and Stephen Drury Smith, eds. *Say It Plain: A Century of Great African American Speeches.* New York: New, 2005.

Ellsberg, Robert. *All Saints: Daily Reflections on Saints, Prophets, and Witnesses for Our Time.* New York: Crossroad, 1997.

Ellul, Jacques. *The Technological Bluff.* Grand Rapids: Eerdmans, 1990.

Epictetus. *The Art of Living: The Classical Manual on Virtue, Happiness, and Effectiveness.* New York: HarperCollins, 1995.

Fadulu, Lola. "Study Shows Income Gap Between Rich and Poor Keeps Growing, with Deadly Effects." *New York Times*, September 10, 2019. https://www.nytimes.com/2019/09/10/us/politics/gao-income-gap-rich-poor.html.

Fisher, Roger, and William Ury. *Getting to Yes: Negotiating Agreement without Giving In.* New York: Penguin, 1983.

Forni, P.M. *Choosing Civility.* New York: St. Martin's, 2002.

Foster, Richard. *Celebration of Discipline: The Path of Spiritual Growth.* New York: HaperCollins, 1998.

———. *Streams of Living Water: Celebrating the Great Traditions of Christian Faith.* New York: HarperCollins, 1998.

Foster, Richard, and James Bryan Smith, eds. *Devotional Classics.* New York: HarperCollins, 1993.

Fowler, James W. *Stages of Faith: The Psychology of Human Development and the Quest for Meaning.* New York: HarperCollins, 1981.

Frankel, Viktor E. *Man's Search for Meaning.* New York: Pocket, 1974.

Fry, Timothy, et al. *The Rule of St. Benedict in English.* Collegeville, MN: Liturgical, 1981.

Gilbert, Elizabeth. *Big Magic: Creative Living Beyond Fear.* New York: Riverhead, 2015.

Gottman, John M., and Nan Silver. *The Seven Principles for Making Marriage Work.* New York: Three Rivers, 1999.

Helliwell, J., Layard, R., and Sachs, J. *World Happiness Report 2019.* New York: Sustainable Development Solutions Network.

Heschel, Abrhama Joshua. *I Asked for Wonder: A Spiritual Anthology.* Edited by Samuel H. Dresner. New York: Crossroad, 1993.

Hyde, Catherine Ryan. *Pay It Forward.* New York: Simon and Schuster, 1999.

Irving, Debby. *Waking up White: And Finding Myself in the Story of Race.* Cambridge, MA: Elephant Room, 2014.

Iyer, Pico. *The Art of Stillness: Adventures in Going Nowhere.* New York: Simon and Schuster, 2014.

Jantsch, Erich. *The Self-Organizing Universe: Scientific and Human Implications of the Emerging Paradigm of Evolution.* Oxford: Pergamon, 1980.

Jones, E. Stanley. *Mahatma Gandhi: An Interpretation.* Nashville: Abingdon-Cokesbury, 1958.

———. *The Way: 364 Daily Devotions.* Nashville: Abingdon, 2015.

Joshi, Mantu. *The Resilient Parent: Everyday Wisdom for Life with Your Exceptional Child.* Pottsboro, NC: DRT, 2013.

Kabat-Zinn, Jon. *Coming to Our Senses: Healing Ourselves and the World Through Mindfulness.* New York: Hyperion, 2005.

Keating, Thomas. *Intimacy with God: An Introduction to Centering Prayer.* New York: Crossroad, 2019.

King, Martin Luther, Jr. *MLK at Western.* Kalamazoo, MI: Western Michigan University Archives, 1963.

———. *Letter from Birmingham Jail.* London: Penguin, 2018.

———. *Strength to Love.* Philadelphia: Fortress, 1963.

King, Maxwell. *The Good Neighbor: The Life and Work of Fred Rogers.* New York: Abrams, 2018.

Kretzmann, John, and John McKnight. *Building Communities from the Inside Out: A Path Toward Finding and Mobilizing a Community's Assets.* Chicago: ACTA, 1993.

Kripalani, Krishna, ed. *All Men Are Brothers: The Life and Thoughts of Mahatma Gandhi as Told in His Own Words*. New York: World Without War, 1972.

Kushner, Harold. *Practice Random Acts of Kindness: Bring More Peace, Love, and Compassion into the World*. San Francisco: Conari, 2007.

Kuttner, Robert. "Blaming Liberalism." *The New York Review of Books*, November 21, 2019.

Lakoff, George, and Mark Johnson. *Metaphors We Live By*. Chicago: University of Chicago Press, 1980.

Le Guin, Ursula K. *Lao Tzu: Tao Te Ching: A Book about the Way and the Power of the Way*. Boston: Shambhala, 2009.

———. *The Unreal and the Real: Selected Stories*. Easthampton, MA: Small Beer, 2012.

Leslie, Ian. *Curious: The Desire to Know and Why Your Future Depends on It*. New York: Basic, 2014.

Levine, Madeline. *The Price of Privilege: How Parental Pressure And Material Advantage Are Creating A Generation Of Disconnected And Unhappy Kids*. New York: HarperCollins, 2006.

Loeb, Paul Rogat, ed. *The Impossible Will Take a Little While: A Citizen's Guide to Hope in a Time of Fear*. New York: Basic, 2004.

———. *Soul of a Citizen: Living with Conviction in Challenging Times*. New York: St. Martin's Griffin, 1999.

MacAfee, Norman, ed. *The Gospel According to RFK: Why It Matters Now*. Boulder, CO: Perseus, 2004.

Machado, Antonio. *Fields of Castile/Campos de Castilla: A Dual-Language Book*. Translated by Stanley Appelbaum. Mineola, NY: Dover, 2007.

Mandell, Fred, and Kathleen Jordan. *Becoming a Life Change Artist: 7 Creative Skills to Reinvent Yourself at Any Stage of Life*. New York: Penguin, 2010.

Maslow, A.H. *The Farther Reaches of Human Nature*. New York: Penguin, 1976.

Mason, John. *Conquering an Enemy Called Average*. Tulsa, OK: Insight, 1996.

McCarthy, Niall. "U.S. Hate Crimes Remain At Heightened Levels." *Statista*, November 13, 2019. https://www.statista.com/chart/16100/total-number-of-hate-crime-incidents-recorded-by-the-fbi/.

McLaren, Brian. *We Make the Road by Walking: A Year-Long Quest for Spiritual Formation, Reorientation, and Activation*. New York: Jericho, 2014.

McLaughlin, Corrine, and Gordon Davidson. *Spiritual Politics: Changing the World from the Inside Out*. New York: Ballantine, 1994.

Meacham, Jon. *The Soul of America: The Battle for Our Better Angels*. New York: Random House, 2018.

Merton, Thomas. *The Inner Experience: Notes on Contemplation*. New York: Harper Collins, 2003.

———. *Thoughts in Solitude*. New York: Farrar, Straus and Giroux, 1958.

Needleman, Jacob. *The American Soul: Rediscovering the Wisdom of the Founders*. New York: Penguin Putnam, 2002.

Nhat Hanh, Thich. *How to Sit*. Berkeley: Parallax, 2014.

———. *Silence: The Power of Quiet in a World Full of Noise*. New York: HarperOne, 2015.

Niebuhr, Reinhold. *The Irony of American History*. Chicago: University of Chicago Press, 2008.

Nouwen, Henri J.M. *Here and Now: Living in the Spirit*. New York: Crossroad, 2006.

———. *Reaching Out: The Three Movements of the Spiritual Life.* New York: Doubleday, 1975.

———. *Spiritual Formation: Following the Movements of the Spirit.* New York: HarperCollins, 2010.

Oates, Stephen B. *Let the Trumpet Sound: The Life of Martin Luther King, Jr.* New York: New American Library, 1982.

O'Donohue, John. *Anam Cara: A Book of Celtic Wisdom.* New York: HarperCollins, 1997.

———. *To Bless the Space Between Us: A Book of Blessings.* New York: Doubleday, 2008.

Orwell, George. *Animal Farm.* New York: Penguin, 1996.

Palmer, Parker. *Healing the Heart of Democracy: The Courage to Create a Politics Worthy of the Human Spirit.* San Francisco: Jossey-Bass, 2011.

———. *A Hidden Wholeness: The Journey Toward an Undivided Life.* San Francisco: Jossey-Bass, 2004.

Pennington, Basil. *Centering Prayer: Renewing an Ancient Christian Prayer Form.* New York: Doubleday, 2001.

Prothero, Stephen. *Whose America Is This? How Our Words Unite, Divide, and Define a Nation.* New York: HarperCollins, 2012.

Putnam, Robert, and Lewis Feldstein. *Better Together: Restoring the American Community.* New York: Simon and Schuster, 2003.

Putnam, Robert. *Bowling Alone: The Collapse and Revival of American Community.* New York: Simon and Schuster, 2000.

Rand, Ayn. *The Virtue of Selfishness.* New York: Signet, 1964.

Rasmus, Rudy. *Love. Period.: When All Else Fails.* Brentwood, TN: Worthy, 2014.

Rogers, Frank, Jr. *Practicing Compassion.* Nashville: Upper Room, 2015.

———. *The Way of Jesus: Compassion in Practice.* Nashville: Upper Room, 2016.

Rohr, Richard. *Just This: Prompts and Practices for Contemplation.* Albuquerque, NM: CAC, 2017.

———. "Transforming Pain." *Center for Action and Contemplation* (blog). October 17, 2018. https://cac.org/transforming-pain-2018-10-17/.

Roosevelt, Eleanor. *Tomorrow Is Now: It Is Today That We Must Create the World of the Future.* New York: Penguin, 2013.

Roth, John K., ed. *The Moral Philosophy of William James.* New York: Thomas Y. Crowell, 1969.

Sacks, Jonathan. *The Dignity of Difference: How to Avoid the Clash of Civilizations.* London: Continuum, 2002.

Saul, John Ralston. *On Equilibrium: Six Qualities of the New Humanism.* Toronto: Penguin, 2001.

Schein, Edward. *Humble Inquiry: The Gentle Art of Asking Instead of Telling.* San Francisco: Berrett-Koehler, 2013.

Schroeder, C. Paul. *Practice Makes Purpose: Six Spiritual Practices That Will Change Your Life and Transform Your Community.* Minneapolis, MN: Hexad, 2017.

Schweitzer, Albert. *Out of My Life and Thought.* New York: Henry Holt, 1933.

Shaffer, Carolyn R., and Kristin Anundsen. *Creating Community Anywhere: Finding Support and Connection in a Fragmented World.* Los Angeles: Jeremy P. Tarcher, 1993.

Sheehy, Gail. *New Passages: Mapping Your Life Across Time.* New York: Random House, 1995.

Skocpol, Theda. *Diminished Democracy: From Membership to Management in American Civic Life.* Norman, OK: University of Oklahoma Press, 2003.

Smith, Huston, with Jeffery Paine. *Tales of Wonder: Adventures Chasing the Divine.* New York: HarperCollins, 2009.

Sparks, Allister, and Mpho Tutu. *Tutu: Authorized.* New York: HarperCollins, 2011.

Spier, Peter. *People.* New York: Doubleday, 1980.

Spink, Kathryn. *The Life and Vision of Brother Roger of Taizé.* London: SPCK, 1986.

Spretnak, Charlene. *States of Grace: The Recovery of Meaning in the Postmodern Age.* New York: HarperCollins, 1991.

Stafford, William. "Vocation." In *The Way It Is: New and Selected Poems,* 102. Minneapolis: Graywolf, 1999.

Stengel, Richard. *Mandela's Way: Fifteen Lessons on Life, Love, and Courage.* New York: Crown, 2009.

St. James, Elaine. *Inner Simplicity: 100 Ways to Regain Peace and Nourish Your Soul.* New York: MJF, 1995.

Takaki, Ronald. *A Different Mirror: A History of Multicultural America.* Boston: Little, Brown and Co., 1993.

Taylor, Alan. "The Virtue of an Educated Voter." *American Scholar,* September 6, 2016 https://theamericanscholar.org/the-virtue-of-an-educated-voter/.

Thurman, Howard. *Deep Is the Hunger.* Richmond, IN: Friends United, 1951.

———. *Meditations of the Heart.* New York: Harper and Brothers, 1953.

———. *The Search for Common Ground.* New York: Harper and Row, 1971.

———. *With Head and Heart.* New York: Harcourt, Brace and Company, 1979.

Tolstoy, Leo. *What Then Must We Do?* Translated by Aylmer Maude. Cambridge: Green, 1991.

Turkle, Sherry. *Reclaiming Conversation: The Power of Talk in a Digital Age.* New York: Penguin. 2015.

UN General Assembly. *Universal Declaration of Human Rights.* December 10, 1948, 217 A (III).

US Census Bureau. *American Community Survey, 2018.* Prepared by US Department of Commerce.

US Department of Justice. *2018 Hate Crime Statistics.* November 12, 2019. Distributed by the Federal Bureau of Investigation: Criminal Justice Information Services Division.

"US mass killings hit a record high in 2019: 'This seems to be the age of mass shootings.'" *USA Today,* December 28, 2019. https://www.usatoday.com/story/news/nation/2019/12/28/us-mass-shootings-killings-2019-41-record-high/2748794001/.

Vonnegut, Kurt. *Player Piano.* New York: Dial, 2006.

Wallis, Jim. *Faith Works: Lessons from the Life of an Activist Preacher.* New York: Random House, 2000.

———. *The Soul of Politics: A Practical and Prophetic Vision for Change.* New York: New, 1994.

Walsh, Roger. *Essential Spirituality: Exercises from the World's Religions to Cultivate Kindness, Love, Joy, Peace, Vision, Wisdom, and Generosity.* New York: John Wiley and Sons, 1999.

Webb-Mitchell, Brett. *Practicing Pilgrimage: On Being and Becoming God's Pilgrim People.* Eugene, OR: Cascade, 2016.

Wheatley, Margaret J. *Finding Our Way: Leadership for an Uncertain Time.* San Francisco: Berrett-Koehler, 2005.

Bibliography

———. *Perseverance*. San Francisco: Berrett-Koehler, 2010.

———. *Turning to One Another: Simple Conversations to Restore Hope in the Future*. San Francisco: Berrett-Koehler, 2002.

———. *Who Do We Choose to Be? Facing Reality, Claiming Leadership, Restoring Sanity*. Oakland: Berrett-Koehler, 2017.

Williamson, Marianne. *The Healing of America*. New York: Simon and Schuster, 1997.

Woodard, Colin. *American Nations: A History of the Eleven Rival Regional Cultures of North America*. New York: Penguin, 2011.

Woodruff, Paul. *Reverence: Renewing a Forgotten Virtue*. Oxford: Oxford University Press, 2001.

Made in the USA
Middletown, DE
21 December 2020

29895741R00099